TOP Secrets to Create A TOP Performing Business

by Howard L. White, Jr.

Top Secrets to Create A Top Performing Business

Top Secrets to Create A Top Performing Business

COPYRIGHT AND DISCLAIMER

HOWARD L. WHITE, JR.

ISBN: **978-0-578-14098-8**

Published by:
TOP Choice
6960 Goya Ave.
Baton Rouge, LA 70806
Tel: 1 225 924 3700
Fax: 1 225 924 0654
Website: www.noresults-nofee.com

Top Secrets to Create A Top Performing Business

DEDICATION

This book is dedicated to my wife, Janice, for allowing me to explore and borrow time from her and to my son, Lee, who inspires me to be both genuine and authentic. I strive to be better because of you two.

To Your Success,

Howard L. White, Jr.

Top Secrets to Create A Top Performing Business

CONTENTS

Top Secrets to Create A Top Performing Business

INTRODUCTION

Even though I truly believe we are all 1 or 2 great marketing ideas away from more sales opportunities than we can fully imagine. I believe the first two chapters are as important as the remaining chapters. The strategies in this book - when implemented with strategy and care - are guaranteed to make you more money with less effort.

This is the reason I followed my calling to be a Business Coach. As a business coach, my company meet daily with small business owners that have the need for marketing, structure, accountability and for the need to surround themselves with someone that cares and to provide a proper and profitable third party perspective.

It is my goal and objective to provide you with some simple, proven and effective ideas that will help you and your team develop a stronger and more profitable business. From the early chapters that will help you create effective goals for you and your team to the later chapters that will help you to create realistic and dynamic marketing programs to take your business to the next level.

As you follow the book and read the principles, remember it does not matter what industry nor type of business you operate (I've been part of many). What matters is that you grasp the heart of the principles, the underlying lessons and strategies, that can help grow any operation in any category of business imaginable.

The best time to start is NOW, not tomorrow, not next week or next year. The number one reason that you will not succeed is because you fail to execute. We often coach and remind our clients to "Do What You Know and Not What You Feel". This simply means develop your plan and then work your plan. Each chapter and each idea will provide you with several tactics that will help you to implement and execute immediately.

Yours in success,

Howard L. White, Jr.

PS. If you would like to arrange a meeting to get a profitable third party perspective on your business, please send an email to info@topchoicebusinessacademy.com and we will gladly point you in the right direction.

For a Free Test Drive of all my best tips, tricks and marketing resources visit www.topchoicebusinessacademy.com.

To Schedule a complimentary BYB (Boost Your Business) Coaching Session visit www.chatwithhoward.com.

1

Use Goal Setting Effectively

We've all heard about the power of setting goals. Everyone has surely seen statistics that connect goal setting to success in both your business life, and your personal life. I'm sure if I asked you today what your goals are, you could rattle off a few wants and hopes without thinking too long.

However, what most people do not realize is that the power of goal setting lies in *writing goals down*. Committing goals to paper and reviewing them regularly gives you a 95% higher chance of achieving your desired outcomes. Studies have shown that only three to five percent of people in the world have written goals – the same three to five percent who have achieve success in business and earn considerable wealth.

These studies have also found that by retirement, only four per cent of people in the world will have enough accumulated wealth to maintain their income level, and quality of life. As a business owner, it is essential that you develop a plan for your retirement, but it is equally essential that you develop a plan for your success.

This chapter focuses on the power of goal setting as part of your business success. We'll teach you to set SMART goals that are rooted in your own personal value system, and supporting techniques to achieve your goals faster.

What are Goals?

Goals are clear targets that are attached to a specific time frame and action plan; they focus your efforts, and drive your motivation in a clear direction. Goals are different from dreams in that they outline a plan of action, while dreams are a conceptual vision of your wish or desired outcome.

Goals require work; work on yourself, work for your business, and work for others. You cannot achieve a goal – no matter how badly you want it – without being prepared to make a considerable effort. If you are ready to invest your time and energy, goals will help you to:

- Realize a dream or wish for your personal or business life
- Make a change in your life – add positive, or remove negative
- Improve your skills and performance ability
- Start or change a habit – positive or negative

Why Set Goals?

As we've already reviewed, setting goals and committing them to paper is the most effective way to cultivate success. The most important reason to set a goal is **to attach a clear action plan to a desired outcome.**

Goals help focus our time and energy on one (or several) key outcome at a time. Many business owners have hundreds of ideas whirring around in their heads at any one time, on top of daily responsibilities. By writing down and focusing on a few ideas at a time, you can prioritize and concentrate your efforts, avoid being stretched too thin, and produce greater results.

Since goals attach action to outcomes, goals can help to break down big dreams into manageable (and achievable) sections. Creating a multi-goal strategy will put a road map in place to help you get to your desired outcome. If your goal is to start a pizza business and make six figures a year, there are a number of smaller steps to achieve before you achieve your end result.

Success doesn't happen by itself. It is the result of consistent and committed action by an individual who is driven to achieve something. Success means something different for everyone, so creating goals is a personal endeavor. Goals can be large and small, personal and public, financial and spiritual. It is not the size of the goal that matters; what matters is that you write the goal down and commit to making the effort required to achieve it.

What happens when I achieve a goal?

You should congratulate yourself and your team, of course! By rewarding yourself and your team after every achievement, you not only train your mind to associate hard work with reward, but develop loyalty among your employees.

You should also ask yourself if your achievement can be taken to the next level, or if your goal can be stretched by building on the effort you have already made. Consistently setting new and higher targets will lay the framework for constant improvement and personal and professional growth.

Power of Positive Thinking

When was the last time you tuned into your internal stream of consciousness? What does the stream of thoughts that run through your mind sound like? Are they positive? Negative? Are they logical? Reasonable?

Top Secrets to Create A Top Performing Business

Positive thinking and healthy self-talk are the most important business tools you can ever cultivate; by programming a positive stream of subconscious thoughts into your mind, you can control your reality, and ultimately your goals. Think about someone you know who is constantly negative; someone who complains and whines and makes excuses for their unhappiness. How successful are they? How do their fears and doubts become reality in their world?

You are what you continuously believe about yourself and your environment. If you focus your mind on something in your mental world, it will nearly always manifest as reality in your physical world.

Positive thinking is a key part of setting goals. You won't achieve your goal until you believe that you can. You will achieve your goals faster when you believe in yourself, and the people around you who are helping to make your goal a reality.

Successful people are rooted in a strong belief system – belief in themselves, belief in the work they are doing, and belief in the people around them. They are motivated to improve and learn, but also confident in their existing skills and knowledge. Their positive attitude and energy is clearly felt in everything they do.

Ever notice how complainers usually surround themselves with other complainers? The same is true of positive thinkers. If you cultivate an upbeat and positive attitude, you will be surrounded by people who share your values and outlook on life.

Too often, people and our society subscribe to a continuous stream of negative chatter. The more you hear it, the more you'll believe it.

How many times have you heard:

- That's impossible.
- Don't even bother.
- It's already been done.
- We tried that, and it didn't work.
- You're too young.
- You're too old.
- You'll never get there.
- You'll never get that done.
- You can't do that.

Positive thinking and positive influences will provide the support you need to achieve your goals. Choose your friends and close colleagues wisely, and surround yourself with positive thinkers.

Creating SMART Goals

SMART goals are just that: smart. Whether you are setting goals for your personal life, your business, or with your employees, goals that have been developed with the SMART principle have a higher probability of being achieved.

The SMART Principle

1. Specific

Specific goals are clearer and easier to achieve than nonspecific goals. When writing down your goal, ask yourself the five "W" questions to narrow in on what exactly you are aiming for. Who? Where? What? When? Why?

For example, instead of a nonspecific goal like, "get in shape for the summer," a specific goal would be, "go to the gym three times a week and eat twice as many vegetables."

2. Measurable

If you can't measure your goal, how will you know when you've achieved it? Measurable goals help you clearly see where you are, and where you want to be. You can see change happen as it happens.

Measurable goals can also be broken down and managed in smaller pieces. They make it easier to create an action plan or identify the steps required to achieve your goal. You can track your progress, revise your plan, and celebrate each small achievement. For example, instead of aiming to increase revenue in 2009, you can set out to increase revenue by 30% in the next 12 months, and celebrate each 10% along the way.

3. Achievable

Goals that are achievable have a higher chance of being realized. While it is important to think big, and dream big, too often people set goals that are simply beyond their capabilities and wind up disappointed. Goals can stretch you, but they should always be feasible to maintain your motivation and commitment.

For example, if you want to complete your first triathlon but you've never run a mile in your life, you would be setting a goal that was beyond your current capabilities. If you decided instead to train for a five mile race in six months, you would be setting an achievable goal.

4. Relevant

Relevant – or realistic – goals are goals that have a logical place in your life or your overall business strategy. The goal's action plan can be reasonably integrated into your life, with a realistic amount of effort.

For example, if your goal is to train to climb to base camp at Mount Everest within one year and you're about to launch a start-up business, you may need to question the relevance of your goal in the context of your current commitments.

5. Timely

It is essential for every goal to be attached to a time-frame – otherwise it is merely a dream. Check in to make sure that your time-frame is realistic - not too short, or too long. This will keep you motivated and committed to your action plan, and allow you track your progress.

Autosuggestion + Visualization

Autosuggestion and visualization are two techniques that can assist you in achieving your goals. Some of the most well-known and successful people in the world use these techniques, and it is not coincidence that they are masters in their own fields of business and sport. A few of these people include:

- Michael Phelps (Olympic Swimmer)
- Andre Agassi (Tennis)
- Donald Trump (Real Estate)
- Wayne Gretzky (Hockey)
- Bill Gates (Microsoft)
- Walt Disney (Entertainment)

Of course, each of these people have a high degree of talent, ambition, intelligence and drive. However, to reach the top of their respective field, they have each used Autosuggestion and Visualization.

Autosuggestion

Autosuggestion is your internal dialogue; the constant stream of thoughts and comments that flows through your mind, and impacts what you think about yourself and how you perceive situations.

Since you were a small child, this self-talk has been influenced by your experiences and has programmed your mind to think and react in certain ways. The good news is that you can reprogram your mind and customize your self-talk any way you like. That is the power of Autosuggestion.

To begin practicing Autosuggestion, make sure you are relaxed and open to trying the technique; an ideal time is just before bed, or when you have some time to sit quietly. Then, repeat positive affirmations to yourself about the ideal outcome. Top sports and business people will often practice just before a big game or meeting.

Some examples of positive self-talk or autosuggestion include:

- I will lead my team to a victory tonight!
- I will be relaxed open to meeting new people at the party tonight!
- I will deliver a clear and impacting speech!
- I will stop worrying and tackle this problem tomorrow!
- I will stand up for my own ideas in the meeting!
- I will remember everything I have studied for the test tomorrow!

Visualization

Visualization is a practice complementary to Autosuggestion. While you can repeat affirmations to yourself over and over, combining this practice with visualization is twice as powerful.

Visualization is exactly what it sounds like: repeatedly visualizing how something is going to happen in your mind's eye. Nearly everyone in sports practices this technique. It has been proven to enhance performance better than practice alone.

This technique can easily be applied to business. For example, prior to any presentation or meeting where you must speak, present or "perform." You can also visualize yourself being incredibly productive and effective in your office. Or, having a discussion with your spouse calmly and rationally.

Elements to think about during visualization:

- What does the room look like?
- What do the people in the room look like?
- What is their mood? How do they receive me?
- What image do I project?
- How do I look?
- How do I behave? What is my attitude?
- What is the outcome?

2

How to Profit through Time Management

Manage Time Like Money

Why did you get into business for yourself? Was it to be your own boss? Choose your own hours? Have more time with the family? Spend more time doing what you love? Chances are, you answered yes to all these questions.

These days, you probably wonder where the time went. Why you spent 12 hours at work and barely make a dent in your to-do list. We already know that time is a key resource for you and your business, but it's also a key resource in your life. Harnessing and leveraging time is the only way to enjoy life, and have a profitable business at the same time.

Most business owners carefully manage their financial and personnel resources, and pay due attention to their performance. Marketing plans and budgets are created, people are hired and fired.

What most business owners don't realize is that time – and the time of all employees – requires the same attention and diligent management.

Time will never manage itself. The decision to make a pro-active effort to manage your time must come from you. Once you have committed to taking ownership for your own time management, there are a host of tools available to you. But first, you must understand how much your time is actually worth, and where you are currently spending it.

What is Your Time Worth?

Ever wonder what your time is actually worth? Here's a quick way to figure it out:

Target annual income	A.
Working days in a year	B. 235
Working hours in a day	C. 7
Working hours in a year	D. 1,645
A ÷ D = YOUR HOURLY WORTH (before tax + expenses)	E.

This is a very simple calculation intended to put your time in perspective. In reality, no one is productive for each of the 1,645 hours. Various studies have put actual productivity at anywhere between 25 minutes and four hours per day. Either way, there's a lot of room for improvement.

Let's look at it another way:

Your age	A.
Days in a year	B.
Days spent on earth to date (A x B)	C.
Average life expectancy	D. 70
Total projected days on earth (D x B)	E.
Estimated days left (E – C)	F.

This exercise isn't intended to scare you, but bring your attention to the importance of choosing how you spend each hour you have available. It is a choice! By developing the skills required to manage your time, you will not only have a profitable business, but a rewarding and balanced life.

The Five Culprits of Time Theft

Chances are – if you're like most people – you have no idea where your time goes. You're likely frustrated by the fact that you can spend 10, 12, even 14 hours a day working, and not make a dent in your to-do list, or only bill half of those hours.

Top Secrets to Create A Top Performing Business

When we're too busy and overloaded with work, we often switch into reactive mode. We can't make it to the bottom of the pile, and end up handling issues and making decisions at the last minute. One of the great benefits of choosing to become proactive in time management is that you can become proactive in all other areas of your business. When in proactive mode, you can take steps to grow your business through networking, building programs, and establishing systems.

Before you investigate where your time goes, let's take a look at the top five culprits of modern-day time theft:

1. Your Email

How many times a day do you check your email? Is Outlook or Mail constantly running on your desktop? Email – internal, external, personal and business – clogs up your day like no other communication channel. For many of us, it is possible to spend the entire day writing and responding to emails without even glancing at our inbox. The number of emails sent and received each day by the average person in 2007 was 147. Multiply that by an average of two minutes per message, and you have spent almost five hours one email in a single day.

2. Your SMART Phone

Smart phones have created convenience, security, and the luxury of telecommuting –smart phones have also created a society that expects to be able to reach you at any moment, or at least receive instant responses to their calls. Your smart phone not only robs you of your time during the day, but also during the evenings and on weekends when you are not at work.

3. Your Open Door Policy

If you make it easy for your staff and associates to interrupt you, they will. Too often, open-door policies are set up by human resource departments to create clear communication channels. Instead, they create a clog of employees lined up at your door seeking immediate answers to non-emergent issues.

4. Meetings

How many times have you been to a meeting that was scheduled to be an hour, and ended up lasting three? How often do you attend unnecessary meetings? Or meetings that run off-topic? Meetings can be a huge source of wasted time – your valuable time. In a senior management or ownership position, your day may consist of back-to-back meetings, leaving only your evening hours to complete the tasks that should have been done during the day.

5. YOU!

Every person has daily habits that sabotage their ability to work productively and efficiently. Many entrepreneurs and business owners can't separate business hours from leisure hours. Some get caught in a time warp while surfing the internet. Others - mainly overachievers – can become paralyzed by perfectionism or procrastination. Mainly we just don't have the tools to schedule and structure our time in a way that fits with our working style.

Where Does Your Time Go?

So far we've seen that time is a resource that should be as carefully managed as cash, we've figured out what your time is worth, and looked at the top five culprits of time theft. You've committed to taking steps to become a better time manager. What now?

Personal Time Management Research Exercise

The next step is to take a good, (and honest!) look at how you spend your time. Once you understand your patterns and habits, you begin to implement the strategies in this chapter that will make you a better time manager.

Step One: Time Audit

Use the Time Log Worksheet at the back of this chapter to record how you spend your time for three working days in a row. Be honest, and be specific. Include time spent in transit, surfing the web, interacting with clients and colleagues, as well as how your time is spent at home in the evenings. The more information you can record, the easier it will be to analyze your time management skills in step two.

Step Two: Time Categorization

Once you have recorded your time for three days, sit down with all three sheets in front of you and identify the following using different colored markers or highlighters:

- Driving, public transportation or other travel
- Eating, including food preparation

- Personal Errands
- Exercise
- Watching TV
- Sleeping, including naps
- Using the computer, personal use only
- Being with family / friends
- Emailing, including checking, reading, and returning messages
- Talking on the phone, including checking and returning messages
- Internal meetings
- External meetings
- Administrative work
- Client work
- Non-client, non-administrative work

Step Two: Time Analysis

Now that you have identified how you have spent your time, go through the worksheets one more time and identify if you have spent enough, too much, or too little time on each main task.

Then, based on your observations, answer the following questions:

Top Secrets to Create A Top Performing Business

1. What patterns do you notice about how you spend your time during the day? (i.e., When are you most productive? Least productive? Most or least interrupted?)

_____

_____

_____

_____

_____

_____

_____

_____

2. Write down the four highest priorities in your life right now. Does your timesheet reflect these priorities?

_____

_____

_____

_____

_____

3. If you have more time, what would you do?

_____

_____

_____

4. If you had less time, what wouldn't you do?

_____

_____

_____

_____

5. Could you remove the items in question four and add the items in question three? Why or why not?

_____

_____

_____

_____

_____

6. Is procrastination a problem for you? How much?

_____

_____

_____

_____

_____

Strategies for Profitable Time Management

There are many ways to curb time theft and refine your time management ability. Through a solid understanding of how you currently spend – and waste – time, you can determine which strategies you need to implement to correct unproductive behavior.

Here are 17 ways you can turn **less** of your time into **more** money:

1. Set Clear Priorities

The foundation of time management a clear understanding of what your time is best spent on. Once you accept that you can't do everything, you need to decide what needs to be completed now, what can be completed later, and what someone else can complete. Each to-do list you create should be put through this filter, and reorganized so the highest priority items are on top, and the lowest priority items are less visible, or on the bottom.

Once you have established your priorities – which will also naturally reflect the priorities and goals of your business – stick to them. Just because someone else feels something is of a high priority doesn't mean it holds the same status next to your other tasks.

Prioritization is also helpful in your personal life and leisure time. Your spare time is precious – so make sure are clear on how you would like to spend it.

2. Use Your Skills – Delegate Your Weaknesses

As a business owner, your day naturally consists of tasks you dislike doing. Some are essential – signing checks, reviewing financial statements, and other business maintenance – while others are simply not within your skill set.

If you are a strong public speaker, but struggle with report writing – delegate to a copywriter or editor. If you own a retail store and have no experience in design – outsource your signage. These freelance professionals often cost half as much as you, and take half as long to complete the task. Your time is saved for tasks that use and strengthen your skills effectively, your stress is managed, and ultimately a better product is produced.

3. Delegate, Delegate, Delegate

As a small business owner, the only way you will ever get everything done is by delegating. Delegation is a vital skill that needs to be refined and practiced, and once mastered is the key to profitable time management.

Top Secrets to Create A Top Performing Business

Too often, owners and managers believe that it will be "faster" or "more efficient" to complete the task themselves than to train and monitor someone else. Other times, there are no internal resources to download assignments to.

As a result, the following trends can be seen in many small companies:

- Owners and senior staff are stressed and overworked, while junior staff are underutilized and under capacity.

- Staff members are not given an opportunity to grow and develop in their roles, and may perceive a lack of trust or confidence in their ability. The company loses good people.

- Owners and senior staff are always in a reactive state, instead of a visionary or proactive state.

- Delegation happens at the very last minute, and junior staff has little understanding of either the overall project or expectations for the task.

The easiest way to fix this problem is before it starts. Create a solid team of staff members around you who are well-trained and prepared to support the business. Attract and retain qualified and quality people who can be cross-trained and promoted within the company. Ensure that communication flows throughout the business, so everyone has the product and service knowledge to step in and assist when necessary.

4. Learn to Say "No"

It's easy to fall into the habit of saying yes to everything. You are, after all the business owner, right? No one can complete these tasks as well as you, right? You'll lose that customer if you don't help them with their garage sale, right?

Wrong. The most successful business owners have a keen understanding of how their time is best spent, and *delegate* the remaining responsibilities to trusted others. It's too easy to say yes to every request in the moment, and later feel overwhelmed when it's added to your to do list. You may not ruffle any feathers, but what toll does it take on your stress level? Your workload? Your time is valuable – so protect it!

Remember that if it is too challenging to say no immediately, you can always request some time to think about it. This way, you can evaluate your workload and realistically decide whether or not you can take on a new project. Then, stand by your decision, or assist in bringing in the necessary resources to get it done.

5. Create (and keep!) a Strict Schedule

While multi-tasking is a desirable skill, it is also often a time thief. Attempting to do too many things at one time ensures that nothing gets done. As a business owner, you need to be able to focus and concentrate on essential projects without interruptions.

The only way to do this is the commit to a strict schedule. Once you understand your work style and concentration patterns, you can allocate periods of the day to specific tasks. This includes personal and leisure time – schedule it, and stick to it.

Schedule time for: list-creation + prioritization, email messages, telephone messages, internal meetings, client meetings, meeting preparation, "me-time", family time, recreation + fitness, daily business tasks, and blocks for focused work.

Remember that there is a training period involved in beginning a new routine – for yourself and those around you. Use your voicemail, out-of-office email message, and a closed door to begin to let people know when you will not be disturbed.

6. Make Decisions

The choice to not make a decision is a decision in itself. The most successful business owners have the ability to make good decisions quickly and efficiently, and do not waste time deliberating over simple choices.

In leadership positions, often people are afraid of making the wrong decision or looking foolish if they make a mistake in front of junior staff. What they don't realize, is that hesitating or avoiding decision making impacts their leadership just as much or more than making the wrong decision. Not only can being indecisive be personally stressful, but it is also stressful for those around you whose tasks are waiting on your choices.

Remember, you must make the best decision with the information you have, in the time frame you have to make the decision. No one expects you to be a fortune teller – be decisive, make some mistakes, and learn from them.

7. Manage Telephone Interruptions

This is a huge source of time theft that can easily be managed and avoided. If you are available to take phone calls at any time of day, you are setting yourself up to take work home in the evenings. The phone will always ring when you are focused on an important task, and this is something can easily be avoided.

Figure out when you are most productive. Is it in the morning or the afternoon? Before, during, or after lunch? Once you have identified this time period, set your phone on "do not disturb" or have your calls directed to voicemail. If you do not have a receptionist, a variety of automatic answering systems are available for a nominal fee. To structure your phone time further, let callers know on your voicemail what specific time of day is best to reach you via phone. Then, set that time aside to receive and return phone calls.

8. Keep Your Work Environment Organized

Have you ever tried to make dinner in a messy kitchen? More of your time is spent looking for (and cleaning) dishes and tools than actually spent cooking the meal.

The same goes for your work environment. If your desk and office is in a constant state of chaos, then you mind will be too. In fact, some studies have revealed that the average senior business leader spends nearly four weeks each year navigating through messy or cluttered desks, looking for lost information. Does that sound like productive time to you?

Top Secrets to Create A Top Performing Business

Once you make the initial clean sweep, it's easy to maintain order in the chaos:

- Tidy your desk at the beginning and end of each day. Attach pertinent documents to your to do list, or have clear and organized folders for loose papers.
- Organize your supplies drawer so you have easy access to stationery like pens, post-it notes, staplers and highlighters. Every minute counts!

- Only have the documents and files you are working on, on your desk. The rest should be neatly filed on a side table for later retrieval.

- Keep personal items (like photos or memorabilia) out of your primary line of vision. These can be distracting and encourage daydreaming.

As for your office or store, there are many ways to make its layout more conducive to effective time management. Try:

- Minimizing the distance between the reception desk and electronics like photocopies and fax machines.

- Keep a clear line of sight between your office and the most productive area of your business, so you are aware of what is happening amongst your staff.

- Organize shelves and filling cabinets so files are not only easily accessed, but out of sight when not being used. Consider putting sliding doors or cabinets in storage areas, and remember that the floor is not a storage cabinet.

9. Keep Your Filing System Organized

If your data isn't organized properly, you will waste hundreds of hours searching for documents you need on a regular basis. This includes both electronic and hard copy files; they need to be organized and up to date.

Customer databases and enquiry records are worth their weight in gold. You can't afford to get behind when updating this information, or poorly store it for later retrieval. There are many easy to use software programs that will manage and organize customer databases for you; it doesn't need to be a time consuming or tedious exercise.

A simple way to manage information is to keep it in short, medium, and long term files for both hard and electronic copies. Create shortcuts on your desktop for folders or files you constantly access. Have short-term files available on your desk, medium-term files available within an arm's reach, and long-term files stored in cabinets.

10. Clearly Communicate – Never Assume

One of the biggest issues for time management in business – and likely the world – is miscommunication. This is a dangerous issue that can cripple any business, including yours. Establishing and enforcing clear policies on things like accurate note taking, task assignments, and phone messages will ensure your staff understand the importance of clear and accurate communication.

The easiest habit to start to curb miscommunication is simple: write everything down. Carry a notepad, and jot down key points, figures, agreements and deadlines. Don't assume you'll remember later – you have at least a hundred other things to remember.

Some other simple strategies are:

- Return all communication promptly, including email, letters, faxes and phone calls

- Repeat back phone messages, phone numbers and other figures to confirm you recorded the information correctly.

- Record appointments in your SMART PHONE or agenda the moment you make them. Otherwise, you will forget.

- Double check and confirm everything – addresses, phone numbers, meeting locations and times.
- Maintain accurate customer contact logs with dates, times, and phone numbers.

- Post checklists in your store or office for routine operations procedures.
- Announce any changes to the policies and procedures manual immediately.

11. Stop Duplicating Efforts

This is a key element of time management that is closely related to effective communication. Studies have continually shown that many businesses often duplicate and triplicate efforts that need only be completed once.

When you have clear systems and procedures in place, your staff will not need to "reinvent the wheel" each time the task needs to be completed. Meeting minutes and individual task assignments will ensure everyone is on the same page and understands their personal responsibilities.

Simple examples of this include re-reading your to-do list each hour to determine what the next important item is. If your list is already structured by priority, this is a needless task. If two staff members are working on similar projects, but unaware of the other, the work will not only be inconsistent, but the efforts will be duplicated. These are easy problems to fix, once they have been identified and communicated.

12. Say Goodbye to Procrastination + Perfectionism

Procrastination is something we all face at one time or another – and likely have since our school days. However, given the pace that the world operates at today, you will only fall behind your competitor if you allow procrastination to rule your day. So how you do avoid it? It's simple. Stop, and just get started, no matter how boring, tedious, or painful the project may be. Reward yourself by crossing each step off your to-do list.

Many small business owners also fall victim to perfectionism, which can be paralyzing. The fear that there isn't enough time or resources to "get it perfect" will sometimes stop you dead in your tracks. Perfectionism can also hinder your ability to delegate and say no to tasks you believe no one else can complete "better". Do the best you can with the time and resources you have – and just get started.

13. Plan Your Work, Work Your Plan

Have you ever placed an advertisement on the fly because it was "cheaper", "faster", or "more urgent" than creating a marketing plan? Do you and your staff have a clear idea of where your business is headed over the next six to 12 months, or five years?

Many studies show that less than 10% of small businesses have up to date marketing and business plans, as compared to the majority of large corporations and public companies, which have both.

Marketing and business plans take time and effort to create – but they work, and pay off in spades. They also save you time and money as compared to a haphazard or fly-by-the-seat-of-your-pants strategy. With a marketing plan in place, you will have an idea of how many ads you will be placing in a year, which will earn you a volume discount. Your marketing materials will complement each other, and deliver the same message to the same target audience. Designers will charge less for a package of collateral than for individual collateral items.

A business plan will provide you with a guide to reference when making decisions. You can repeatedly ask if the endeavor at hand will contribute to your overall vision, or just seems like a good idea or price.

Remember that planning includes both short and long-term time frames, and applies to both your daily to-do list, and your marketing budget. It provides you with a means to measure your progress, assists in identifying priorities, and helps to manage your time.

14. Avoid Needless, Impromptu + Unstructured Meetings

This may seem like a time theft issue that is out of your control, but it's not. You are in control of your own time, and through strict scheduling can establish a structure for internal and external meetings that everyone around you can work within.

Minimize impromptu internal meetings by letting your staff know when you're available for a "quick chat" and when you are not. If it is important, ask them to schedule a time to meet with you that works with both of your schedules. This not only saves you time, but encourages staff to find solutions to their own issues, and only approach you with more urgent or challenging matters.

You can't avoid having meetings, but you can avoid having unstructured meetings. Ask for or create an agenda for each meeting you attend, with a clear objective and an amount of time allocated to each item. This will keep your meetings focused and on task. If a meeting does run late, give yourself a reasonable buffer, and politely leave for your next appointment. You can always follow up with a colleague to catch-up on the pertinent items you may have missed.

15. Establish Clear Policies + Procedures

A clear policy and procedures manual is like a marketing or business plan – it takes time to create, but ultimately saves everyone in your company time, money and effort. A step-by-step guide to "the way we do things here" is an invaluable resource for your existing and new staff, and provides clear expectations for how you like things done.

Too many businesses make up policies and procedures on the fly – creating dangerous scenarios where mistakes are made and expectations are not clear. Some items that should be included in a comprehensive policy and procedures manual include:

- Recruitment
- Customer relations
- Customer enquiries
- Customer complaints

- Returns
- Exchanges
- Late Payments
- Salary structure
- Bonus structure
- Employee review
- Theft
- Harassment

16. Keep the Right Set of Tools

The equipment your business needs to operate (and grow!) effectively should always be on hand, or easily contracted out. This is specific to each company, and closely related to costs – including the cost of your time.

Whether you are a high-tech business or local retailer, knowledge of the latest advancements in technology will increase your efficiency. It will help you stay on top of the competitor, maintain your position as an expert, and perhaps provide an easier way of getting things done.

Always ask yourself if these purchases are essential to your business –could perhaps make these purchases from a second hand dealer to minimize cost? Is it more cost effective to outsource or sub-contract the tasks to someone with access to this equipment, or to buy the equipment yourself?

If your business relies on tools and technology for daily tasks (such as the trades profession) then obtaining the best quality you can afford is crucial.

17. Maintain Your Equipment

This may seem obvious, but you'll understand the importance if your network server has ever crashed, or point of sale system has malfunctioned. Your business can be slowed to a stand-still if your equipment is not in good working order. Of course there are instances that can't be predicted, but regular maintenance of your essential equipment will reduce these occurrences and help to anticipate when old equipment needs to be repaired or replaced.

Personal Time Management Strategy

Choose the top five tips from this chapter that you think will help you the most, given your personal time management research. Write them below, with three corresponding actions that you will start tomorrow. For example, if you are going to set a strict schedule, three

Top Secrets to Create A Top Performing Business

actions might be to establish the schedule, communicate it to your staff, and re-record your voicemail message.

1. _____

    a. _____

    b. _____

    c. _____

2. _____

    a. _____

    b. _____

    c. _____

3. _____

    a. _____

    b. _____

    c. _____

Top Secrets to Create A Top Performing Business

4. _____

    a. _____

    b. _____

    c. _____

5. _____

    a. _____

    b. _____

    c. _____

www.topchoicebusinessacademy.com

Timesheet | Day One

Timeslot	Activities	More/Less/ Enough time?
7:00 – 7:30		
7:30 – 8:00		
8:00 – 8:30		
8:30 – 9:00		
9:00 – 9:30		
10:00 – 10:30		
10:30 – 11:00		
11:00 – 11:30		
11:30 – 12:00		
12:00 – 12:30		
12:30 – 1:00		
1:00 – 1:30		
1:30 – 2:00		
2:00 – 2:30		
2:30 – 3:00		
3:00 – 3:30		
3:30 – 4:00		
4:00 – 4:30		
4:30 – 5:00		
5:00 – 5:30		
5:30 – 6:00		
6:00 – 10:00 (Evening)		

Timesheet | Day Two

Timeslot	Activities	More/Less/ Enough time?
7:00 – 7:30		
7:30 – 8:00		
8:00 – 8:30		
8:30 – 9:00		
9:00 – 9:30		
10:00 – 10:30		
10:30 – 11:00		
11:00 – 11:30		
11:30 – 12:00		
12:00 – 12:30		
12:30 – 1:00		
1:00 – 1:30		
1:30 – 2:00		
2:00 – 2:30		
2:30 – 3:00		
3:00 – 3:30		
3:30 – 4:00		
4:00 – 4:30		
4:30 – 5:00		
5:00 – 5:30		
5:30 – 6:00		
6:00 – 10:00 (Evening)		

Timesheet | Day Three

Timeslot	Activities	More/Less/ Enough time?
7:00 – 7:30		
7:30 – 8:00		
8:00 – 8:30		
8:30 – 9:00		
9:00 – 9:30		
10:00 – 10:30		
10:30 – 11:00		
11:00 – 11:30		
11:30 – 12:00		
12:00 – 12:30		
12:30 – 1:00		
1:00 – 1:30		
1:30 – 2:00		
2:00 – 2:30		
2:30 – 3:00		
3:00 – 3:30		
3:30 – 4:00		
4:00 – 4:30		
4:30 – 5:00		
5:00 – 5:30		
5:30 – 6:00		
6:00 – 10:00 (Evening)		

Daily To-Do List | Business

Task	Priority (1-10)	Deadline?	Delegation?

Weekly To-Do List | Personal (Family, Leisure, etc.)

Task	Priority (1-10)	Deadline?	Delegation?

3

How to Organize Your Office for Success

Have you ever tried to cook a fancy gourmet dinner in a messy kitchen?

It starts out okay. I have all the ingredients I need; it just takes me a little longer to find them as I go. I have to find and clear some counter space, then wipe the crumbs off of it and grab a knife.

Some pots are clean, so I use them first. But then I need the double boiler, and it's still crusted with last night's meal, so I have to wash it. While I'm washing the pot, the garlic and onion that I'm sautéing starts to burn, so I have to run over and rescue it.

Pretty soon, I'm running around like crazy, trying to rescue each item I cook because I'm busy preparing what I need for the next dish. It should be no surprise that the meal was a disaster.

Your place of work is just like your kitchen. It needs to be clean, well-organized, and ready to function. Your tools need to be prepared and at the ready in order to support the tasks you and your staff need to complete.

A well set-up office – with all the necessary tools – will save you time and the expense of redundancy. This is the first key to an effective and successful business operation.

Create an Office for Profitability

Most people understand the relationship between time management and profitability. Effective time management increases productivity; more work can be completed in less time, with less distraction and waste.

Office organization also affects profitability and productivity. A tidy and well-structured office is not only a more pleasant place to work, but it also reduces the time anyone might spend looking for items and digging through loose paperwork.

A well-organized office also encourages better internal communication. There are clear areas of the business that are designated for sales news, target tracking, and project planning. This fosters team building and collaborative work ethic.

Getting Started: Workspace Audit

The best place to start is by taking an honest inventory of the current state of your office or working environment. With that information, you can determine what areas need to be improved, streamlined, or de-cluttered. Spend some time taking a look around your office and note the following:

- Is there a location where internal company information is displayed?
- What is the distance between your office and the printer or photocopier?
- How much lose paper is found around the business?
- What is hung up on the walls?
- Do your staff members have organization systems for their own desks?
- What can be found on your desk?
- How many files are used on a daily or weekly basis?
- Where are old or outdated files kept?

Organize Your Desk

Presumably, your desk is where you spend the most time in your office. It is where you are expected to be the most productive. To get all your important tasks completed.

Top Secrets to Create A Top Performing Business

Simply put, you will be more productive and effective if your workspace is clean and organized. Spend some time each day tidying and organizing your workspace – ideally when you are planning your work or your schedule for the following day.

Here are some other ways you can keep your immediate workspace in the most productive form possible:

Phone. Put your phone on the left side of the desk if you are right handed and on the right side of the desk if you are left handed. Keep a notebook by the phone to record messages and conversation notes. Also record phone messages here, and delete them from your system.

Personal Items. Keep person items out of your immediate line of sight. Pictures can be distracting, and points for daydreaming.

Organizer. Keep your Planner or Smart Phone easily accessible on your desk. Use this as your main system for notes, tasks, follow-up, and brainstorming. Keep the rest of your desk clear.

Files. Only keep the files you need on your desk or within arm's reach. Store any files you don't use daily or weekly in a filing cabinet further away.

Inbox and action items. Sort items in your inbox into an easily accessible file sorter or a stack of paper trays. Separate paper into the following categories: to-do, to-review, waiting response, on-hold, to file.

Organize Your Office

Take the information you gathered in your workplace audit and identify opportunities for improvement. Can the office benefit from a better layout? A paper management system? More clearly defined areas? A new filing system?

The answer will depend on the unique needs of your business, and take into account how you and your staff use the space. Here are some suggestions and guidelines for improving the organization of your office or place of business:

Establish Clear Areas

Divide your office into areas of productivity, and locate all related materials and equipment in each area.

Here are some sample areas you may wish to consider:

- Printing and photocopying
- Office supplies
- Financial paperwork and accounting
- Team gathering
- Kitchen or food-related preparation
- Reception
- Point of sale

Create a Central Location for Information

Many people – including your employees – learn and interpret information that is visual better than any other means of communication. A central location in your office for staff to go for company information and updates is an essential tool for team building and internal communications.

Every office needs:

Whiteboard

Place a whiteboard in an easily accessed place – your staff communication center or the boardroom. This whiteboard is for brainstorming, project planning, marketing planning, or any other use that may be required.

This is a great tool for team meetings, client meetings, and management meetings. The facilitator can diagram information and work through issues on the spot.

Sales Board

Create a customized sales board for your business. Take a whiteboard, and some thin black tape, and create a chart or diagram that records regular sales statistics and targets.

You may wish to separate the whiteboard into two sections – target sales and actual sales, and compare based on weekly, quarterly, and yearly targets. You can also compare actual sales to sale for the same period the previous year.

12-Month Marketing Planner

Chart your marketing plan on a large calendar and post it in a central area. This is a clear reminder of the big picture, and each of the promotions you have planned over the course of the year.

Remember to write in dry-erase marker so you can easily make changes. Consider color-coding your promotions or projects for easy visibility.

Manage Paper + Filing

System	Steps
Create a master filing system and color code it	Group vendor files (accounts payable) and assign a color Group client files (accounts receivable) and assign a color Group project or product files and assign a color
Sort each filing category by date or alphabetically by name	Sort vendor or supplier files by name Sort client files by client number or name Sort project files by project number or name
Create a binder of master lists for regularly accessed information	Office passwords Financial accounts Goals Birthdays Vendor contact information
Use a bound notebook	Keep track of phone calls and messages Put the date on each page Eliminate loose notepaper
Get rid of magazines and other reading material	Throw away industry magazines and newspapers Keep relevant articles of interest Sort them into files, if necessary
Keep tax-related documents in one spot	File all receipts, donations and other tax related information in the same filing cabinet Make copies of documents you need to file in more than one spot
Create a business care management system	Throw away old business cards Organize cards by last name or company name in a binder or rolodex Enter the information in a data management program, then throw away the cards

4

Profits Through Building a TEAM
(Together Everyone Achieves More)

The people you employ contribute – directly or indirectly – on a daily basis to the strength and vitality of your business. You can't run your business alone, so you rely on their skills and support.

In simpler words, your employees help you to make money.

But your employees are not just the people who arrive at your office every day and exchange effort for a paycheck. Their role is not just to build capacity and sell more or serve more.

Your employees are part of a potentially powerful group of people that you can leverage to put your business on the fast track to success. Your staff is more than the people who work for you. They are actually members of your team – the group of people who are collectively working to achieve the same objective, or reach the same vision.

I say they are more than just employees because their collective, cohesive value is actually much higher than their individual worth.

We all know that more people working on the same task will ensure the task is completed faster. In business, when you have more people working together on the same task, you save time, increase brainpower, and ultimately, **make more money**.

Corporate Culture

Corporate Culture has become a common buzzword when it comes to building a successful business, and rightly so.

Your corporate culture is the environment in which you run your business, and the environment in which your team members work. It is rooted in the vision, mission and beliefs of the organization, and dictates the "kind of office" and "kind of people" that work in that office.

Corporate culture is something that typically develops organically. The business owner and senior employees create a positive or negative environment based solely on who they are as people and how they behave as leaders. You simply can't avoid creating some type of corporate culture when you run a business.

Top Secrets to Create A Top Performing Business

You can, however, avoid creating a negative or unproductive corporate culture. Whether you are just starting out, or seeking to improve your workplace, you do have control over the type of environment in which you run your business.

Like most things in business, this won't happen overnight. However, with a clear idea of where you want to go, and what you want to create, you'll be well on your way to getting there.

Vision

Your company's vision statement should be a bold, clear, short sentence that every single one of your employees knows and understands. It is a roadmap to your idea of success; if you don't know what that looks like, how will you know when you achieve it?

If your goal is to create a highly profitable company – what does highly profitable mean? $1 million in annual sales?$3 million in annual profit?

Do you seek to become the industry leader in sprocket production? How will this be measured? How many sprockets will you have to produce to reach this goal?

Top Secrets to Create A Top Performing Business

The vision statement is a short summary of the long-term objective of the company. What the company will look like, produce, achieve; it is how you know the company is "successful."

Many companies either do not have a vision statement or they keep it a secret from their employees. It is only discussed in board meetings or management meetings. For a team to collectively work toward a goal, they need to know what the big picture objective is. They need to have buy-in in the company's direction, and be communicated with on a regular basis.

Be proud of your vision. Keep it visible for staff – post it on the wall, include it in internal communications, and connect day to day activities too it as often as possible.

Sample Vision Statements

Here are some real examples of corporate vision statements:

"At Microsoft, our mission and values are to help people and businesses through the world realize their potential." – Microsoft

"Give every customer a reason to believe...STAPLES Business Depot—That was easy!" – Staples Canada

Top Secrets to Create A Top Performing Business

"To build the largest and most complete Amateur Radio community site on the Internet." – eHam.net

Creating a Vision Statement

The process of creating a vision statement is something that you can work through alone, or in collaboration with your team. It is highly recommended to review the draft vision statement with your employees to ensure they understand and support the goals and objectives of the company.

Keep the following points in mind when crafting your vision statement:

- **Think big** – Why did you start or buy this business? What was your dream or purpose in doing so?
- **Think long-term** – Vision statements should last five to 10 or even 25 years
- **Be specific** – Use numbers, dates, ratings systems and other ways of measuring success
- **Be succinct** – Use clear, short, simple sentences that are easy to repeat and remember

Top Secrets to Create A Top Performing Business

Mission

Your mission statement is a general description of how you are going to achieve your vision. This is a longer and more detailed statement that should include what your business is, who your customers are, and how you are different from (better than!) the competition.

Sample Mission Statements

"The Mission of McGill University is the advancement of learning through teaching, scholarship and service to society: by offering to outstanding undergraduate and graduate students the best education available; by carrying out scholarly activities judged to be excellent when measured against the highest international standards; and by providing service to society in those ways for which we are well-suited by virtue of our academic strengths." – McGill University, Montreal, Canada

"Starbucks purchases and roasts high-quality whole bean coffees and sells them along with fresh, rich-brewed, Italian style espresso beverages, a variety of pastries and confections, and coffee-related accessories and equipment -- primarily through its company-operated retail stores. In addition to sales through our company-operated retail stores, Starbucks sells whole bean coffees through a

specialty sales group and supermarkets. Additionally, Starbucks produces and sells bottled Frappuccino® coffee drink and a line of premium ice creams through its joint venture partnerships and offers a line of innovative premium teas produced by its wholly owned subsidiary, Tazo Tea Company. The Company's objective is to establish Starbucks as the most recognized and respected brand in the world." – Starbucks

Creating Your Mission Statement:

Here is a recommended process for completing your mission statement:

Step One: List your company's core strengths and weaknesses; what do you do well? What do you need to work on, or avoid doing?

Step Two: Who are your primary customers? Describe the types of customers you serve – both internal and external.

Step Three: What do your customers think of your strengths? What strengths are most important to them? Go ahead and ask them if you need to.

Step Four: Connect the strength that each customer values with its customer type. Write it in a sentence. Combine any redundancies.

Step Five: Organize your sentences in order of importance

Step Six: Combine your sentences into a paragraph or two. Elaborate on points as needed. This is your draft mission statement.

Step Six: Consult with your staff and customers, and ask for their feedback. Do employees support the statement? Can they act on it? Do customers want to do business with a company with this mission statement? Does it make sense?

Step Seven: Incorporate the feedback received, and refine the statement until you are happy with it. Then publish it – everywhere.

Culture or Values Statements

Your culture or values statement is the next step in the process. It describes how you and your staff will go about taking action (your mission statement) to achieve your objective (your vision statement).

Much like every family has their own belief system and way of doing things – from cooking to cleaning to raising kids – every company has their own set of values when it comes to running a business. It reflects the unique personality of the organization.

Sample Culture Statement

Our Culture

* Values-based leadership. Our Credo outlines the values that provide the foundation of how we act as a corporation and as individual employees so that we continue to put the needs of the people we serve first.

* Diversity. It's our individual differences that make us stronger as a whole. We recognize the strength and value that comes when collaborative relationships are built between people of different ages, race, gender, religion, nationality, sexual orientation, physical ability, thinking style, personal backgrounds and all other attributes that make each person unique.

* Innovation. True innovation can only be fostered within a supportive environment that values calculated risk in order to achieve the maximum reward. At Johnson & Johnson Inc., we encourage and reward innovative thinking, innovative solutions and an innovative approach in all that we do.

Top Secrets to Create A Top Performing Business

* Passion. The deep desire to enrich people's lives – by delivering quality products and remarkable experiences that make their lives easier, healthier and more joyful.

* Collaboration. The unwavering belief that great results depend on the ability to create trusting relationships.

* Courage. The fearless pursuit of the unproven, unknown possibility – the willingness to take great risks for the benefit of the greater good.

- Johnson & Johnson Canada

Creating Your Culture Statement

Involve your team in creating your company's culture or values statement. Generally, this is a point-form document that reflects the beliefs of the company, its employees, and its customers.

It can be helpful to think about the type of people you currently employ, as well as the ones you may wish to employ. What are they like? What are their belief systems? What are their most important values?

Remember that the culture or values statement is usually the longest of the three statements – and that's okay.

Your Team Leaders

The strength of a team lies in the strength of the people who lead it. No group of people is effective without strong leadership, just like no business is effective without a strong owner or management team.

Building a strong team means knowing who your leaders are – both in job description and natural ability.

Understanding the strength of your natural leaders and the skills of your natural followers will allow you to strategically structure your team for maximum effectiveness and efficiency. It will give you insight into who is best suited for management promotions and project management; which team members have the ability to assemble and motivate their peers.

Your leaders need to have a high degree of passion for your product or service, and truly believe in the company's vision. They need to be able to handle a high level of responsibility, and manage a range of people to achieve a common goal.

Your leaders are your team builders. They present new ideas, build consensus, and encourage the involvement of others.

Top Secrets to Create A Top Performing Business

Types of Leaders

Simply speaking, there are four main types, or styles, of leaders. Chances are, you've experienced each type at some point in your career.

Type	Description	Ideal Use
Autocratic	Classical or "old-school" approach Manager holds all power and decision-making authority No employee consultation or input Orders are obeyed Rewards/punishment structure	New, untrained employees Detailed orders and instructions are required No other leadership style has been effective Limited time available Department restructuring High production requirements
Bureaucratic	"By the book" approach All is done to specific procedures/policies All tasks outside policies referred to higher management	Routine tasks performed Standards and procedures need to be communicated regularly Safety or training Cash handling Dangerous equipment

Top Secrets to Create A Top Performing Business

Laissez-faire	"Hands-off" approach Employees have almost total freedom Little direction or guidance is provided Employees must make own decisions, set own goals Employees must solve own problems	Highly skilled and experienced employees Employees are highly driven and ambitious Consultants are being managed Employees are trustworthy
Democratic	"Participatory approach" Employees part of decision making process Employees well informed Leader has final say, but involved others Collaborative approach Encourages employee development with guidance and assistance from leader Leader recognizes and rewards achievement	Collaborative environment Employee development and growth is the focus Changes or problems affect employees and require their input to create a solution Team building and participation is encouraged

Communication

The only way to build and maintain a strong team is through strong, consistent communication. This is often an overlooked or neglected aspect of business management, and is easily forgotten during periods of high stress or heavy workload.

Avoid letting communication fall on the backburner by creating a regular meeting schedule – and sticking to it. Depending on the size and type of your business, daily, weekly, or monthly team meetings are an important cornerstone of a strong team.

Regularly scheduled team meetings are like Sunday dinners with a busy family. They give you – the owner – a regular forum with your staff to implement company-wide training initiatives, announce results, establish goals and targets, or share new visions or directions. They also give your staff a forum to share feedback and air grievances.

Effective Team Meetings

By now you're probably thinking, "Sure, I hear some company's team meetings are effective, but we tried them and it didn't work," or "I held regular team meetings, but after a while, no one showed up."

Top Secrets to Create A Top Performing Business

There is a difference between team meetings held for the sake of having team meetings, and well prepared team meetings with a purpose.

You need to start holding team meetings with a purpose.

Establish a Schedule That Everyone Can Commit To

Scheduling is potentially the biggest challenge when trying to set up a team meeting. Often, all of your staff members are busy going in eight different directions to fulfill their roles and operating on dramatically different schedules.

This is one reason why regular team meetings are important. Ad hoc meetings require ad hoc scheduling, and reduce the likelihood that all your team members will be able to attend.

Ask your team to block off one hour (or two) each week (or month) for the team meeting in a time slot that is convenient for everyone. Establish a clear attendance expectation from everyone. This will exclude that time slot from the scheduling of other meetings and avoid conflict.

If you find that a team meeting is not necessary one week, you can always cancel it.

Top Secrets to Create A Top Performing Business

Know Your Purpose

Each team meeting should have a purpose and clear objectives. Is it to educate? Build consensus? Gather feedback?

Once you have established a purpose for a particular meeting, send an agenda to your staff confirming the meeting and outlining your objectives. This is a good time to ask if anyone has a subject they would like to raise at the meeting.

If you find you do not have a clear purpose or objective, ask yourself if a team meeting is the best use of time for that week and consider postponing it to the next regularly scheduled time slot.

Plan Each and Every Minute

The biggest complaint from employees about team meetings is the length. Too often team meetings run out of control, and end up taking three hours instead of one. You will quickly lose team focus and respect for the regular meeting this way. By establishing a clear agenda and staying on topic, you can run an efficient, succinct meeting.

Your detailed agenda should include:

- meeting purpose or objective
- list of topics and associated speakers
- list of decisions that need to be made/agreed to
- time allocation for each topic
- opportunity for additional topics at the end

Circulate your draft agenda in advance of the meeting, and request input and feedback. When all team members have reviewed and contributed to the agenda, you will increase their level of ownership and buy-in into the process.

Establish the Facilitator

Choose one person to chair the meeting and keep it on track. This is generally the business owner or a senior member of the team with some authority over junior staff and a high level of respect.

It is the responsibility of the facilitator – or chairperson – to create an environment of open dialogue and trust, and to keep the meeting on schedule.

Create a Follow-up Schedule

Assign the task of taking detailed meeting minutes to a team member – or rotate this responsibility on a regular basis. It is important to record what happens in team meetings, just as you would in a client-related business meeting.

In the minutes, establish a system for tracking the action items that arise from decisions made in the meeting. This can be set up as a simple chart: **D.A.R.T.**

Decision	Action	Responsibility	Timeline

Make sure that these responsibilities are assigned and agreed upon in the meeting, and clear deadlines are established. Reviewing or following up on this chart can serve as a regular topic during team meetings.

Circulate meeting minutes to all attendees and ask for input or revisions. You may wish to circulate meeting minutes with the agenda for the next team meeting, and gather feedback at the same time.

Motivations + Incentives

A big challenge in team building is coming up with new ways to foster and maintain a high level of motivation. How do you keep teams of people excited and driven to succeed over long periods of time? How do you keep your team motivated to improve their performance, and increase their achievements?

It is important to note that we're not just talking about individuals, but teams of people working together. It is fairly simple to motivate a single person, but an entire team of motivated people will generate significantly higher results.

The key here is to give incentives for individual and team accomplishments. Incentives that reward based on collective achievement require people to work together and motivate each other to succeed.

Before we start talking about monetary and incentive-based rewards, it's important to look at motivational factors that are not incentive-driven.

Top Secrets to Create A Top Performing Business

Room to Work

Employees who feel their managers and supervisors believe and trust in their abilities are happier and will always perform at a higher level than those who do not. They are motivated to "prove them right" and feel supported in their efforts.

Micromanagement quickly reduces morale. It is essential that you and your managers clearly express confidence in your team members. You hired them to do a job, perform a role, so you must ensure they have the space to do so.

When you put effective systems in place and establish clear expectations, you create a clear context or boundary system for employees to work within. They understand the decision-making hierarchy, and the general way 'things are done around here.'

Your team should be encouraged to take initiative and to take risks within this context. You have hired your team based on their skills and intellectual capabilities, and thus should be able to trust in their choices and decision making abilities.

Top Secrets to Create A Top Performing Business

Incentives

Incentives are great motivators. An incentive is a reason to perform or act in a certain way. For example, if your team increases sales by 40% by month's end, they will be treated to an expensive dinner.

Incentives need to be specific and have deadlines in order to be effective. In the example above, sales need to increase by 40% by the end of the month in order for the team to receive their dinner. If sales only increase by 30%, or if they increase by 40% at the end of the second month, the team does not earn their reward.

Time-specific incentives increase the sense of urgency, and encourage staff to work harder to achieve the objective. If the incentive is not time-bound, there is no reason to work faster or harder, since staff will assume they will reach their milestone "eventually."

Rarity is also a key component of effective incentive-based team building. If the reward is ongoing (i.e., if staff receive an expensive dinner every month sales are over $75,000), then "there's always next time." There is a lesser incentive to push performance to receive the reward. Some team members may care one month, but not the next.

Monetary Incentives

Bonuses and salary increases are a popular way to give your team an incentive to perform. These can include:

- Commissions
- Bonuses for completing a challenging project, or hitting a target
- Rewards for highest producing employee
- Salary increases based on met targets

It's up to you how you choose to structure your monetary incentives, based on your budget and resources. Remember to ensure that the terms of each incentive are clearly outlined, and that both parties (you and your employee) understand the agreement.

Gift Rewards

Physical, tangible gifts are an inexpensive way to reward your team for achievements and improvement. These rewards show that you have given some level of thought to what they might enjoy or appreciate in exchange for a job well done. They're also a great way to surprise employees.

Top Secrets to Create A Top Performing Business

Here are some ideas:

- Spa gift certificates
- Books – *consider motivational or business-related topics*
- CDs or DVDs
- Meals – lunch or breakfast
- Other gift certificates – gas, food, meals, local shops
- Movie or theatre tickets
- Weekend getaway – hotel, meals, etc.
- Flowers
- Gym memberships

5

Define Your Target Market

What is a Target Market?

Many businesses can't answer the question: *Who is your target market?* They have often made the fatal assumption that *everyone* will want to purchase their product or service with the right marketing strategy.

A target market is simply the group of customers or clients who will purchase a specific product or service. This group of people all have something in common, often age, gender, hobbies, or location.

Your target market, then, are the people who will buy your offering. This includes both existing and potential customers, all of whom are motivated to do one of three things:

- Fulfill a need
- Solve a problem
- Satisfy a desire

To build, maintain, and grow your business, you need to know who your customers are, what they do, what they like, and why they would buy your product or service. Getting this wrong – or not taking the time to get it right – will cost you time, money, and potentially the success of your business.

The Importance of Knowing Your Target Market

Knowledge and understanding of your target market is the keystone in the arch of your business. Without it, your product or service positioning, pricing, marketing strategy, and eventually, your business could very quickly fall apart.

If you don't intimately know your target market, you run the risk of making mistakes when it comes to establishing pricing, product mix, or service packages. Your marketing strategy will lack direction, and produce mediocre results at best. Even if your marketing message and unique selling proposition (USP) are clear, and your brochure is perfectly designed, it means nothing unless it arrives in the hands (or ears) of the right people.

Determining your target market takes time and careful diligence. While it often starts with a best guess, assumptions cannot be relied on and research is required to confirm original ideas. Your target market is not always your ideal market.

Once you build an understanding of who your target market is, keep up with your market research. Having your finger on the pulse of their motivations and drivers – which naturally change – will help you to anticipate needs or wants and evolve your business.

Types of Markets

Consumer

The Consumer Market includes those general consumers who buy products and services for personal use, or for use by family and friends. This is the market category you or I fall into when we're shopping for groceries or clothes, seeing a movie in the theatre, or going out for lunch. Retailers focus on this market category when marketing their goods or services.

Institutional

The Institutional Market serves society and provides products or services for the benefit of society. This includes hospitals, non-profit organizations, government organizations, schools and universities. Members of the Institutional Market purchase products to use in the provision of services to people in their care.

Business to Business (B2B)

The B2B Market is just what it seems to be: businesses that purchase the products and services of other business to run their operations. These purchases can include products that are used to manufacture other products (raw or technical), products that are needed for daily operations (such as office supplies), or services (such as accounting, shredding, and legal).

Reseller

This market can also be called the "Intermediary Market" because it consists of businesses that act as channels for goods and services between other markets. Goods are purchased and sold for a profit – without any alterations. Members of this market include wholesalers, retailers, resellers, and distributors.

Determining Your Target Market

Product / Service Investigation

The process for determining your target market starts by examining exactly what your offering is, and what the average customer's motivation for purchasing it is. Start by answering the following questions:

Top Secrets to Create A Top Performing Business

Does your offering meet a basic need?	
Does your offering serve a particular want?	
Does your offering fulfill a desire?	
What is the lifecycle of your product / service?	
What is the availability of your offering?	
What is the cost of the average customer's purchase?	
What is the lifecycle of your offering?	
How many times or how often will customers purchase your offering?	
Do you foresee any upcoming changes in your industry or region that may affect the sale of your offering (positive/negative)?	

Top Secrets to Create A Top Performing Business

Market Investigation

- **On the ground.** Spend some time on the ground researching who your target market might be. If you're thinking about opening a coffee shop, hang out in the neighborhood at different times of the day to get a sense of the people who live, work, and play in the neighborhood. Notice their age, gender, clothing, and any other indications of income and activities.

- **At the competition.** Who is your direct competitor targeting? Is there a small niche that is being missed? Observing the clientele of your competition can help to build understanding of your target market, regardless of whether it is the same or opposite. For example, if you own a children's clothing boutique and the majority of middle-class mothers shop at the local department store, you may wish to focus on higher-income families as your target market.

- **Online.** Many cities and towns – or at least regions – have demographic information available online. Research the ages, incomes, occupations, and other key pieces of information about the people who live in the area you operate your business. From this data, you will gain an understanding of the size of your total potential market.

- **With existing customers.** Talk to your existing customers through focus groups or surveys. This is a great way to gather demographic and behavioral information, as well as genuine feedback about product or service quality and other information that will be useful in a business or marketing strategy.

Who is Your Market?

Based on your product / service and market investigations, you will be able to piece together a basic picture of your target market, and some of their general characteristics. Record some notes here. At this point, you may wish to be as specific as possible, or maintain some generalities. You can further segment your market in the next section.

Consumer Target Market Framework

Market Type:	Consumer
Gender:	☐ Male ☐ Female
Age Range:	
Purchase Motivation:	☐ Meet a Need ☐ Serve a Want ☐ Fulfill a Desire
Activities:	
Income Range:	
Marital Status:	
Location:	☐ Neighborhood ☐ City ☐ Region ☐ Country
Other Notes:	

Institutional Target Market Framework

Market Type:	Institutional
Institution Type:	☐ Hospital ☐ Non-profit ☐ School ☐ University ☐ Charity ☐ Government ☐ Church
Purchase Motivation:	☐ Operational Need ☐ Client Want ☐ Client Desire
Purpose of Institution:	
Institution's Client Base:	
Size:	
Location:	☐ Neighborhood ☐ City ☐ Region ☐ Country
Other Notes:	

B2B Target Market Framework

Market Type:	Business to Business (B2B)
Company Size:	
Number of Employees:	
Purchase Motivation:	☐ Operations Need ☐ Strategy ☐ Functionality
Annual Revenue:	
Industry:	
Location(s):	
Purpose of Business:	
People, Culture & Values:	
Other Notes:	

Reseller Target Market Framework

Market Type:	Reseller
Industry:	
Client Base:	
Purchase Motivation:	☐ Operations Need ☐ Client Wants ☐ Functionality
Annual Revenue:	
Age:	
Location:	☐ Neighborhood ☐ City ☐ Region ☐ Country
Other Notes:	

Your Target Market: Putting It Together

Based on the information you gather from your product / service and market investigations, you should have a clear vision of your realistic target market. Here are a few examples of how this information is put together and conclusions are drawn:

Target Market Sample 1: Consumer Market

Business: Baby Clothing Boutique	**Business Purpose:** *Meet a need* (provide clothing for infants and children aged 0 to 5 years) *Serve a want* (clothing is brand name only, and has a higher price point than the competition)
Market Type: Consumer	
Gender: Women	
Marital Status: Married	
Market Observations: located on Main Street of Anytown, a street that is seeing many new boutiques open up, proximate to the main shopping mall two blocks from popular mid-range restaurant that is busy at lunch	**Industry Predictions:** large number of new housing developments in the city and surrounding areas two new schools in construction expect to see an influx of new families move to town from Anycity
Competition Observations: baby clothing also available at two local department stores, and one second-hand shop on opposite side of town	**Online Research:** half of Anytown's population is female, and 25% have children under the age of 15 years Anytown's population is expected to increase by 32% within three years The average household income for Anytown is $75,000 annually

.**TARGET MARKET:** The target market can then be described as married mothers with children under five years old, between the ages of 25 and 45, who have recently moved to Anytown from Anycity, and have a household income of at least $100K annually.

Target Market Sample 2: B2B Market

Business: Confidential Paper Shredding	**Target Business Size:** Small to medium
Market Type: B2B (Business to Business)	**Target Business Revenue:** $500K to $1M
Business Purpose: *Meet an operations need* (provide confidential on-site shredding services for business documents)	**Target Business Type:** produce or handle a variety of sensitive paper documentation accountants, lawyers, real estate agents, etc.
Market Observations: there are two main areas of office buildings and industrial warehouses in Anycity three more office towers are being constructed, and will be completed this year	**Industry Predictions:** the professional sector is seeing revenue growth of 24% over last year, which indicates increased client billing and staff recruitment
Competition Observations: one confidential shredding company serves the region, covering Anycity and the surrounding towns provide regular (weekly or biweekly) service, but does not have the capacity to handle large volumes at one time	**Online Research:** Anycity's biggest employment sectors are: manufacturing, tourism, food services, and professional services

.TARGET MARKET:

.The target market can then be described as small to medium sized businesses in the professional sector with an annual revenue of $500K to $1M who require both regular and infrequent large volume paper shredding services.

Segmenting Your Market

Your market segments are the groups within your target market – broken down by a determinant in one of the following four categories:

- Demographics
- Psychographics
- Geographics
- Behaviors

Segmenting your target market into several more specific groups allows you to further tailor your marketing campaign and more specifically position your product or service. You may wish to divide your ad campaign into four sections, and target four specific markets with messages that will most resonate with the audience.

For example, the baby clothing store may choose to segment its target market by psychographics, or lifestyle. If the larger target market is *married females with children under five, between the ages of 25 and 45, who have a household income of at least $100K annually*, it can be broken down into the following lifestyle segments:

- Fitness-oriented mothers
- Career-oriented mothers
- New mothers

With these three categories, unique marketing messages can be created that speak to the hot-buttons of each segment. The more accurate and specific you can make communications with your target market, the greater impact you will have on your revenues.

Market Segmentation Variables

Demographic	Psychographic	Geographic	Behavioristic
Age	Personality	Region	Brand Loyalty
Income	Lifestyle	Country	Product Usage
Gender	Values	City	Purchase
Generation	Attitude	Area	Frequency
Nationality	Motivation	Neighborhood	Profitability
Ethnicity	Activities	Density	Readiness to Buy
Marital Status	Interests	Climate	User Status
Family Size			
Occupation			
Religion			
Language			
Education			
Employment Type			
Housing Type			
Housing Ownership			
Political Affiliation			

Understanding Your Target Market

Once you have determined who your market is, make a point of learning everything you can about them. You need to have a strong understanding of who they are, what they like, where they shop, why they buy, and how they spend their time. Remind yourself that you may *think* you know your market, but until you have verified the information, you'll be driving your marketing strategy blind.

Also be aware that markets change, just like people. Just because you knew your market when you started your business 10 years ago, doesn't mean you know it now. Regular market research is part of any successful business plan, and a great habit to start.

Types of Market Research

Surveys

The simplest way to gather information from your clients or target market is through a survey. You can craft a questionnaire full of questions about your product, service, market demographics, buyer motivations, and so on. Plus, anonymous surveys will produce the most accurate information since names are not attached to the results or specific comments.

Top Secrets to Create A Top Performing Business

Depending on the purpose—whether it is to gather demographic information, product or service feedback, or other data—there are a number of ways to administer a survey.

1. Telephone

Telephone surveys are a more time-consuming option, but have the benefit of live communication with your target market. Generally, it is best to have a third party conduct this type of survey to gather the most honest feedback. This is the method that market researchers use for polling, which is highly reliable.

2. Online

Online surveys are the easiest to administer yourself. There a many web-based services that quickly and easily allow to you custom create your survey, and send it to your email marketing list. These services can also analyze, summarize and interpret the results on your behalf. Keep in mind that the results include only those who are motivated to respond, which may slant your results.

3. Paper-based.

Paper surveys are seldom used, and can prove to be an inefficient method. Like online surveys, your results are based on the feedback of those who were motivated for one reason or another to respond. However, the time and effort involved in taking the survey, filing it out, and returning it to your place of business may deter people from participating.

Keep in mind that surveys can be complex to administer, and consume more time and resources than you have planned. If you have the budget, consider hiring a professional market research firm to lead or assist with the process. This will also ensure that the methodology is standard practice, and will garner the most accurate results.

Website Analysis

Tracking your website traffic is an excellent way to research your existing and potential customer's interests and behavior. From this information, you can ensure the design, structure and content of your website is catering to the people who use it – and the people you want to use it.

User-friendly website traffic analytics programs can easily show you who is visiting your site, where they are from, and what pages of your site they are viewing. Services like Google Analytics can tell you what page they arrive at, where they click to, how much time they spend on each page, and on which page they leave the site.

This is powerful (and free!) information to have in your market research, and easy to monitor monthly or weekly, depending on the needs of your business.

Customer Purchase Data (Consumer Behavior)

If you do not have the budget to conduct your own professional market research, you can use existing resources on consumer behavior. While this data may not be specific to your region or city, general consumer research is actual data that can be helpful in confirming assumptions you may have made about your target market.

Your customer loyalty program or Point of Sale system may also be of help in tracking customer purchases and identifying trends in purchase behavior. If you can track who is buying, what they're buying and how often they're buying, you'll have an arsenal of powerful insight into your existing client base.

Focus Groups

Focus groups look at the psychographic and behavioristic aspects of your target market. Groups of six to 12 people are gathered and asked general and specific questions about their purchase motivations and behaviors. These questions could relate to your business in particular, or to the general industry.

Focus group sessions can also be time consuming to organize and facilitate, so consider hiring the services of a professional market research firm. You may also receive more honest information if a third party is asking the questions, and receiving the responses from focus group participants.

For cost savings, consider partnering with an associate in the same industry who is not a direct competitor, and who would benefit from the same market data.

6

Generating an Unlimited Amount of Leads for Your Business

Where do your customers come from?

Most people would probably choose advertising as an answer. Or referrals. Or direct mail campaigns. This may seem true, but it's not really accurate.

Your customers come from leads that have been turned into sales. Each customer goes through a two-step process before they arrive with their wallets open. They have been converted from a member of a target market, to a lead, then to a customer.

So, would it not stand to reason then, that when you advertise or send any marketing material out to your target market, that you're not really trying to generate customers? That instead, you're trying to generate leads.

When you look at your marketing campaign from this perspective, the idea of generating leads as compared to customers seems a lot less daunting. The pressure of closing sales is no longer placed on advertisements or brochures.

From this perspective, the **general purpose of your advertising and marketing efforts is then to generate leads from qualified customers.** Seems easy enough, doesn't it?

Where Are Your Leads Coming From?

If I asked you to tell me the top three ways you generate new sales leads, what would you say?

- Advertising?
- Word of mouth?
- Networking?
- …don't know?

The first step toward increasing your leads is in understanding how many leads you currently get on a regular basis, as well as where they come from. Otherwise, how will you know when you're getting more phone calls or walk-in customers?

If you don't know where your leads come from, start *today.* Start asking every customer that comes through your door, "how did you hear about us?" or "what brought you in today?" Ask every customer that calls where they found your telephone number, or email address. Then, *record the information for at least an entire week.*

When you're finished, take a look at your spreadsheet and write your top three lead generators here:

1. _____

2. _____

3. _____

From Lead to Customer: Conversion Rates

Leads mean nothing to your business unless you convert them into customers. You could get hundreds of leads from a single advertisement, but unless those leads result in purchases, it's been a largely unsuccessful (and costly) campaign.

The ratio of leads (potential customers) to transactions (actual customers) is called your conversion rate. Simply divide the number of customers who actually purchased something by the number of customers who inquired about your product or service, and multiply by 100.

 # transactions / # leads x 100 = % conversion rate

If, in a given week, I have 879 customers come into my store, and 143 of them purchase something, the formula would look like this: **[143 (customers) / 879 (leads)] x 100 = 16.25% conversion rate**

What's Your Conversion Rate?

Based on the formula above, you can see that the higher your conversion rate, the more profitable the business.

Your next step is to determine you own current conversion rate. Add up the number of leads you sourced in the last section, and divide that number into the total transactions that took place in the same week.

Write your conversion rate here:

_____.

Quality (or Qualified) Leads

Based on our review of conversion rates, we can see that the number of leads you generate means nothing unless those leads are being converted into customers.

So what affects your ability (and the ability of your team) to turn leads into customers? Do you need to improve your scripts? Your product or service? Find a more competitive edge in the marketplace?

Maybe. But the first step toward increasing conversion rates is to evaluate the leads you are currently generating, and make sure those leads are the right ones.

What are Quality Leads?

Potential customers are potential customers, right? Anyone who walks into your store or picks up the phone to call your business could be convinced to purchase from you, right? Not necessarily, but this is a common assumption most business owners make.

Quality leads are the people who are the most likely to buy your product or service. They are the qualified buyers who comprise your target market. Anyone might walk in off the street to browse a furniture store – regardless of whether or not they are in the market for a new couch or bed frame. This lead is solely interested in browsing, and is not likely to be converted to a customer.

A quality lead would be someone looking for a new kitchen table, and who specifically drove to that same furniture because a friend had raved about the service they received that month. **These are the kinds of leads you need to focus on generating.**
How Do You Get Quality Leads?

- **Know your target market.** Get a handle on who your customers are – the people who are most likely to buy your product or service. Know their age, sex, income, and purchase motivations. From that information you can determine how best to reach your specific audience.

- **Focus on the 80/20 rule.** A common statistic in business is that 80% of your revenue comes from 20% of your customers. These are your star clients, or your ideal clients. These are the clients you should focus your efforts on recruiting. This is the easiest way to grow your business and your income.

- **Get specific.** Focus not only on who you want to attract, but how you're going to attract them. If you're trying to generate leads from a specific market segment, craft a unique offer to get their attention.

- **Be proactive**. Once you've generated a slew of leads, make sure you have the resources to follow up on them. Be diligent and aggressive, and follow up in a timely manner. You've done to work to get them, now reel them in.

Get More Leads from Your Existing Strategies

Increasing your lead generation doesn't necessarily mean diving in and implementing an expensive array of new marketing strategies. Marketing and customer outreach for the purpose of lead generation can be inexpensive, and bring a high return on investment.

You are likely already implementing many of these strategies. With a little tweaking or refinement, you can easily double your leads, and ensure they are more qualified.

Here are some popular ways to generate quality leads:

Direct Mail to Your Ideal Customers

Direct mail is one of the fastest and most effective ways to generate leads that will build your business. It's a simple strategy – in fact, you're probably already reaching out to potential clients through direct mail letters with enticing offers.

The secret to doubling your results is to craft your direct mail campaigns specifically for a highly targeted audience of your *ideal* customers.

Your ideal customers are the people who will buy the most of your products or services. They are the customers who will buy from you over and over again, and refer your business to their friends. They are the group of 20% of your clients who make up 80% of your revenue.

Identify your ideal customers

Who are your ideal customers? What is their age, sex, income, location and purchase motivation? Where do they live? How do they spend their money? Be as specific as possible.

Once you have identified who your ideal customers are, you can begin to determine how you can go about reaching them. Will you mail to households or apartment buildings? Families or retirees? Direct mail lists are available for purchase from a wide range of companies, and can be segregated into a variety of demographic and sociographic categories.

Top Secrets to Create A Top Performing Business

Craft a special offer

Create an offer that's too good to refuse – not for your entire target market, but for your ideal customer. How can you cater to their unique needs and wants? What will be irresistible for them?

For example, if you operate a furniture store, your target market is a broad range of people. However, if you are targeting young families, your offer will be much different than one you may craft for empty-nesters.

Court them for their business

Don't stop at a single mail-out. Sometimes people will throw your letter away two or three times before they are motivated to act. Treat your direct mail campaign like a courtship, and understand that it will happen over time.

First send a letter introducing yourself, and your irresistible offer. Then follow up on a monthly basis with additional letters, newsletters, offers, or flyers. Repetition and reinforcement of your presence is how your customer will go from saying, "who is this company" to "I buy from this company."

Top Secrets to Create A Top Performing Business

Advertise for lead generation

Statistics show that nearly 50% of all purchase decisions are motivated by advertising. It can also be a relatively cost effective way of generating leads.

We've already discussed the importance of ensuring your advertisements are purpose-focused. The general purpose of most advertisements is to increase sales – which starts with leads. However ads that are created solely for lead generation – that is, to get the customers to pick up the phone or walk in the store – are a category of their own.

Lead generation ads are simply designed and create a sense of curiosity or mystery. Often, they feature an almost unbelievable offer. Their purpose is not to convince the customer to buy, but to contact the business for more information.

As always, when you are targeting your ideal audience, you'll need to ensure that your ads are placed prominently in publications that audience reads. This doesn't mean you have to fork over the cash for expensive display ads. Inexpensive advertising in e-mail newsletters, classifieds, and the yellow pages are very effective for lead generation.

Top Secrets to Create A Top Performing Business

Here are some tips for lead generation advertising:

Leverage low-cost advertising

Place ads in the yellow pages, classifieds section, e-mail newsletters, and online. If your target audience is technology savvy, consider new forms of advertising like Facebook and Google Adwords.

Spark curiosity

Don't give them all the information they need to make a decision. Ask them to contact you for the full story, or the complete details of the seemingly outrageous offer.

Grab them with a killer headline

Like all advertising, a compelling headline is essential. Focus on the greatest benefits to the customer, or feature an unbelievable offer.

Referrals and host beneficiary relationships

A referral system is one of the most profitable systems you can create in your business. The beauty is once it's set up, it often runs itself.

Top Secrets to Create A Top Performing Business

Customers that come to you through referrals are often your "ideal customers." They are already trusting and willing to buy. This is one of the most cost-effective methods of generating new business, and is often the most profitable. These referral clients will buy more, faster, and refer further business to your company.

Referrals naturally happen without much effort for reputable businesses, but with a proactive referral strategy you'll certainly double or triple your referrals. Sometimes, you just need to ask!

Here are some easy strategies you can begin to implement today:

Referral incentives

Give your customers a reason to refer business to you. Reward them with discounts, gifts, or free service in exchange for a successful referral.

Referral program

Offer new customers a free product or service to get them in the door. Then, at the end of the transaction, give them three more 'coupons' for the same free product or service that they can give to their friends. Do the same with their friends. This ongoing program will bring you more business than you can imagine.

109

Host-beneficiary relationships

Forge alliances with non-competitive companies who target your ideal customers. Create cross-promotion and cross-referral direct mail campaigns that benefit both businesses.

Lead Management Systems

Once your lead generation strategies are in place, you'll also need a system to manage incoming inquiries. You'll need to ensure you receive enough information from each lead to follow up on at a later date. You'll also need to create a system to organize that information, and track the lead as it is converted into a sale.

Gathering Information from Your Leads

Here is a list of information you should gather from your leads. This list can be customized to the needs of your business, and the type of information you can realistically ask for from your potential customers.

- Company Name
- Name of Contact
- Alternate Contact Person
- Mailing Address
- Phone Number
- Fax Number

- Cell Phone
- Email Address
- Website Address
- Product of Interest
- Other Competitors Engage

Top Secrets to Create A Top Performing Business

Lead List Management Methods:

Once you have gathered information from your lead, you'll need a system to organize their information and keep a detailed contact history.

The simplest way to do this is with a database program, but you can also use a variety of hard copy methods.

Electronic Database Programs

- High level of organization available
- Unlimited space for notes and record-keeping
- Data-entry required
- Examples include: MS Outlook, MS Excel, Maximizer
- Customer Relationship Management Software

Index Cards

- Variety of sizes: 3x5, 4X6 or 5X8
- Basic contact information on one side
- Notes on the other side
- Easy to organize and sort

Top Secrets to Create A Top Performing Business

Rolodex System

- Maintain more contacts than index card system
- Easily organized and compact
- Basic contact information on one side
- Notes on the other side
- Can keep phone conversation and purchase details

Notebook

- Best if leads are managed by a single person
- Lots of room for notes
- Inexpensive
- Difficult to re-organize
- Best for smaller lists

Business Card Organizer

- Best for small lists – under 100
- Limited space for notes
- No data entry required
- Rolodex-style, or clear binder pages

7

How to Use Advertising for Immediate Profits

Why do you advertise?

Seems like a silly question, doesn't it? Placing ads in newspapers and on the radio seems like a no-brainer way of growing or maintaining your business. You let a group of people know where your business is and what you sell, and you'll always have customers dropping by, right?

Sure, it's a little more complicated than that. There's your powerful offer, your strong guarantee, the placement of your headline, and how you structure your body copy.

But what I'm really trying to drill down to is *why* you chose to place *that* ad. What is the specific purpose for each advertisement you send out into the world?

Without a solid purpose – or strategy – behind each and every advertisement, it is impossible to measure what is and is not working.

If you placed an ad offering 2 for 1 shampoo one week, and sales for conditioner skyrocketed, would you consider your ad successful? Absolutely not. Sales might have gone up, but the reason you placed the ad was to speed sales on shampoo, which didn't happen.

The point is that each and every advertising dollar should be spent with purpose, focused on a desired outcome and relevant to the big picture. Advertising is expensive! What's the point, unless you're making your money back and then some?

Types of Advertising

There are endless options when it comes to choosing which media to place your advertisements with. The media is a broad and complicated industry, with highly segmented readership.

This can help and hurt your advertising efforts. You have access to highly targeted audiences, but you also may spend a great deal of money on expensive advertising that your target market doesn't go near.

Here are the major types of media advertising:

Print

Print is the most common form of advertising. Ad production is relatively easy and straightforward, and placement is less expensive than broadcast advertising. We'll be focusing on this form of advertising in detail later in the chapter.

Types of print media:

Newspapers – daily and weekly
Magazines
Trade Journals
Newsletters

Radio

Radio advertising reaches a broad audience within a geographic area. This form of advertising can be highly profitable for some businesses, and utterly useless for others. Always consider if there is a simpler, cheaper way of getting your message to your target audience.

Key points to consider for radio advertising:

Use of sounds, voices, tones
Length
Gaining listener's attention
Call to action

Top Secrets to Create A Top Performing Business

Television

Television advertising is largely out of reach for most small business budgets. Creating, developing, and producing TV spots is a costly endeavor, and does not always generate an acceptable return on investment.

This form of advertising generally reaches a broad audience, depending on the timeslot the ad spot airs. Typically, the most expensive airspace is during the region's most popular 6 o'clock news program, or prime time (6pm to 10pm) television line-up.

There are some cost-effective alternatives to TV advertising that you can implement online. You could create a promotional video for your company, and post it on your website and YouTube, or Facebook, or play it in your store. Be creative with your ad budget when it comes to broadcast media.

Online

Online advertising has emerged as an effective tool for your marketing efforts. Internet usage has dramatically increased, and usage patterns have become easier to identify. This form of advertising also allows you to reach a highly qualified audience with minimal investment in ad creation.

Top Secrets to Create A Top Performing Business

Places to advertise online:

Facebook
Google Adwords
Online media (online newspapers and broadcast stations)
Craigslist
Banner ads on complementary websites

Classified

Classified advertising is one of the most highly targeted and cost-effective choices you can make in your overall strategy. People who read classifieds have typically made a decision to buy something, and are looking for places to do so. This is also a great way to test your headlines, offer, and guarantee before you invest in higher-priced advertising.

Classified ad types:

Daily and weekly newspapers
Online
Trade journals

Specific tips for effective classified ads:

- Pick a format for your ad within the specifications of the publication. Will it look like a print display ad? A semi-display ad? A classic line ad? This will affect how you structure your message.

- Choose the category – or two – that best fit with what you have to offer. If two apply, place an ad in both and measure which category generated more leads.

- Grab the attention of your reader with a killer headline, then list benefits, make an irresistible offer, and offer a strong guarantee. Keep the layout simple and ensure the font size is easy to read.

- Notice how other companies are creating their ads, and do something to stand out. The classifieds page is typically cluttered and full of text, so you will need to distinguish your business in some way.
- Use standard abbreviations when creating line ads to maintain consistency. Ask the ad department for a list of abbreviations they typically use.

Niche

Niche advertising can take any of the forms discussed above. The advantage of niche advertising is the super segmentation of each outlet's audience. Typically, there is a very small market in each niche, and a single publication that caters to it. This is very effective for companies who have no need for broad market advertising in traditional or mainstream publications.

Types of niche advertising:

Trade journals
Alternative media
Online blogs
Internal communications – newsletters, etc.

Your Advertising Strategy

Develop a strategy that is purpose driven.

Know exactly why you are choosing advertising, as well as the objective of each and every ad. Compare the benefits of advertising to other promotional strategies like media relations, direct mail, referral strategies and customer loyalty programs.
Some common objectives for advertising strategies include:

- Generate qualified leads
- Increase sales
- Promote new products or services
- Position products or services
- Increase business awareness
- Maintain business awareness
- Complement existing promotional strategies

Top Secrets to Create A Top Performing Business

These objectives will dictate where you advertise, how big each of your advertisements is, and how often you advertise in each outlet.

Find your target audience.

Before you do *anything*, get a solid handle on who your target market is, and each of the segments within it. Think about demographic factors like age, sex, location and occupation, as well as behavioral factors like spending motivations and habits.

The composition of your target audience will be the deciding factor when choosing which media to advertise with, and what to say in each of the advertisements.

Decide on a frequency.

The frequency of your advertising campaign will depend on a number of factors, including budget, purpose, outlet, results, and timing. You may wish to publish a weekly ad that includes a coupon in your local paper. Or, you may only need to advertise a few times a year, just before your peak seasons.

Establish an advertising schedule for the year, or at least each quarter, and plan each advertisement in advance. This will ensure you are not scrambling to place an ad at the last minute, and that each ad is part of an overall proactive strategy instead of a reactive one.

Choose your outlets.

Decide where you are going to advertise and how often in each outlet. You may wish to choose a variety of media to reach several target audiences, or just a large daily newspaper where the most number of people will see it.

It is a good idea when you are starting a new campaign to test its effectiveness in smaller, less expensive publications. Based on the results, you can make changes to the ad and place it in the more expensive outlets.

Remember that although budget is a large factor when deciding on advertising mediums, it is entirely possible to implement a successful ad campaign with minimal cost investment. The key is to make sure that each dollar you spend is carefully thought through – and that your ads are placed in publications that will reach your ideal customers.

Top Secrets to Create A Top Performing Business

Maximize your ad spend with bulk purchases.

If you plan to advertise in a specific publication several times in a given time period, you will benefit from a meeting with the sales representative to review your needs. Often, media outlets will offer discounted rates for multiple placements.

Remember that one company may own several media outlets – including TV, radio, and online media. Ask your sales rep for other discount opportunities when advertising within the ownership group.

Remember to test and measure

How will you know if your campaign is successful if you don't test and measure the results? The only true mistake you can make in advertising is neglecting to track and analyze the results each ad generates.

Get in the habit of keeping a copy of each ad, and record all the details of the placement, including publication, cost, date, response rate, and conversion rate. Many publications will mail you a clipping of your advertisement with your account statement, but don't rely on this as a clipping service.

Evaluate the effectiveness of each ad you place, and learn from what isn't working. If you are advertising in several outlets, make sure asking customers where they saw your ad is part of your incoming phone script and sales script. You will need to monitor not only what types of ads work the best, but also where the ads generate the highest response.

Creating Your Advertisement

You don't need to rely on professional copywriting or design assistance when crafting advertisements from your business. Spend your time and resources on what you are saying, ensure the 'how you say it' is clear, clean, and easy to read.

Ad copy

Headlines
- Take at least half of the time you spend creating your ad, and focus on the headline. Your headline will be the difference between your ad getting read – or not. Boldface your headlines for impact.

- You have about five seconds to grab the reader's attention, so create a headline that sparks curiosity, communicates benefits, or states something unbelievable.

Top Secrets to Create A Top Performing Business

Sub Headlines

- The purpose of your sub headline is to elaborate on your headline, and convince the audience to read the body copy. All the rules of headline writing apply. If you did not mention benefits in your headline, do it in your sub headline. Clearly tell the reader what is "in it for them," and get them reading on.

Body Copy

- Choose your words wisely – you don't have room for lengthy paragraphs. Use bullet points to convey benefits wherever possible, and keep your sentences short. You typically only have about 45 words to convince the customer to keep reading.

- Remember to always include your contact information – phone number and website address at the very least. This seems obvious, but can be forgotten in the design process.

Ad Layout

Size

- Choose your ad size based on the purpose of the ad, and the budget you have available. Larger ads are more expensive, but you do need enough space to communicate your key messages to the audience.

- If you place regular ads to maintain a presence in the local paper, you likely don't need full pages of space. Alternately, if you are launching a new product or service, or having a blowout sale, you will want to buy more space to increase the potential impact.

Graphics

- Graphics should comprise about 25% of your total ad space, and more if you have a small amount of copy. Avoid drawings and clip art. Photographs will generate a better response. Don't underestimate the importance of white space. Give the reader space to "rest" their eyes between headlines and body copy paragraphs.

Font

- Choose clean fonts that are easy to read. Times New Roman and Arial are effective, simple choices. If you use two fonts in your advertisement, make sure you do not combine serif and sans serif fonts, and you keep consistency amongst headers and body copy.

- Ensure that none of your copy is smaller than 9pt. Your audience won't take the time or spend the effort to read tiny copy.

8

How to Use Promotions for Increased Sales Immediately

Promotion and revenue go hand in hand. No matter how long you've been in business, or what kind of company you have; keeping your product/service in the forefront of the consumer's mind is an ongoing process. You want to be the one they remember when they go to buy that hair product or need to get their car fixed.

In simple terms, promotion is about communicating who your company is and enticing your target audience to purchase your product or service. It showcases the marketing messages you put out into the world, and aims to achieve your marketing objectives.

It's an umbrella term that encompasses any activity that is done for the purpose of "getting your name out there" and creating sales. It is one of the main components that make up a marketing plan.

Think big shots like Coca Cola and Microsoft no longer have promotional campaigns? On the contrary, in order to stay at the top of their fields they devote a great deal of energy to promotion; and they keep it going regularly.

If you aren't going to the public, but waiting for them to come to you, you're only creating a one way stream of revenue. In this day and age promotion is a cornerstone of success in business.

Why Everyone Needs to Promote Their Business

We've been discussing how essential marketing plans – and proactive strategies in general - are to success in business. Doing so paints the picture of your company's vision. It forces you to ask yourself what your product/service is all about, and how it will meet your target market's need? The groundwork is laid, but how are you going to communicate this with them? This is where promotion comes into the picture....

You can have the best product in the world....but if the world doesn't know about it, it's not doing anyone any good!

"Getting your name out there" is how you are going to create a strong impression in the minds of your potential customers. One way to get into this style of thinking is to see everything you do as a way to do just that. Sure there are standard methods of promotion which can be very useful, but when you "think outside the box" it can really give you an edge against the competition.

The ways of promotion are endless; all you have to do is get yourself into that mind-set. Once you start thinking like the customer, you'll start to understand what THEY want, and then the opportunities of how to provide it, as well as how to let them know about it, shine through.

Brand Awareness

In a marketplace that is full of variety for consumers to choose from, maintaining a presence and reputation amongst all the other brands and products is essential. This is a term called brand awareness, which really just means getting your company and its product/service known, by repetitive exposure of your marketing messages and logo to the public. Promotion is what allows you to achieve this. It also creates interest and curiosity around your product/service.

Consistent Promotion

Equally important to promoting yourself in general, is promoting on a consistent basis. The effectiveness of doing it suffers if you don't commit to it on a frequent basis. This doesn't have to cost a lot of money, there are plenty of cost-effective methods to choose from.

The goal is to "touch base" with the public. If they gain some brand awareness and then you disappear for a while they'll forget about you, "out of sight, out of mind". If and when you start putting your promotional communications out there it will take a while to catch on again, and plus it looks inconsistent. And as we all know by this point, the key to success in marketing is consistency!

Promotional Strategies

Self-Promotion or Networking

Building relationships is not only the foundation of a success in social situations, but also success in business situations. The two go hand in hand, meaning every situation is a chance to make a potential sale.

Some people feel awkward about showcasing themselves, but no one believes in your product/service more than you do. People sense that genuine enthusiasm and it instills them with confidence. Effective promotion begins with how you promote yourself as an individual.

The key is not to make it the only reason for networking, or at the very least not to let it come across that this is the only reason.

Top Secrets to Create A Top Performing Business

A casual way to create an opportunity to discuss your company is to find out about the other person first. This creates a connection and people are always flattered when you inquire about them. It also gives you the opportunity to learn about their needs and desires. Look for clues of how you could relate your product/service to help them in their life.

When it comes to discussing what "you do for a living" they will be more open to receive your enthusiastic promotion. Even if they don't currently have a need for your product/service they are likely to either keep it in mind for the future, and/or pass that information along to friends and family.

This is how you create a buzz, and the beauty of "word of mouth" is born.

Marketing Promotion

This is used to reach a large number of people simultaneously.

One of the major advantages of using some of these methods is the organic creation of a "brand" for your company. When the messages you are putting out there are consistent, and you provide a product or service of consistent quality, it starts to "make a name" for itself.

Top Secrets to Create A Top Performing Business

For example, Nike doesn't need to write lengthy description of what its products are because they have spent so much effort promoting themselves in the past. Now when you see their little "swoosh" logo, you know which company is being mentioned.

It's pretty hard to achieve that by going door to door talking to your neighbors. Using some of the standard promotion methods to showcase your logo, and expose your company's promotional messages gets you known a whole different level.

Here are some examples of simple and cost-effective promotions:

- **Get your business card into as many hands as possible.** Visit friends and family and leave a small stack of business cards with them to give to others. This can create a tremendous trickle-down effect.

- **Have your company logo professionally painted on your vehicle**

- **Be your own billboard.** Have some shirts printed with you company's info on them and sport one when you're running errands or doing leisure activities. Why not even get a few more made so that friends and family can act as a promo team....free of charge!?

- **Write an article on your area of expertise and submit it to a trade magazine or industry newsletter.** Be sure to include your company's contact information at the bottom.

- **Join a few professional associations and attend meetings and functions as an opportunity to network**

- **Always keep business cards on hand, and give them out throughout the day**

- **Put up flyers on public notice boards/community boards and in related businesses. You can even hand them out on the street!**

Types of Promotions

As previously discussed, you know that promotion is any form of communication regarding your product/service or company. This section discusses the variety of standard promotional methods you can use.

If possible, using a variety of these different types enables you to reach your target market in multiple ways; and since the messages you're putting forward are consistent, this creates a greater impact.

Advertising

This is any form of communication that you pay for. It comes across through another source, but is understood that the message comes from what your company wants the public to know about them.

The following outlets are standard methods of advertising:

- Broadcast: Radio, television, internet
- Outdoor: Billboards, bus shelters and even buses themselves
- Print: Programs for event, newspaper/magazines, trade journals

While advertising is projected to the general public, exposing everyone to your message, you want to ensure that you are targeting a specific market. Its effectiveness is easily lost if you are not choosing an outlet that is accepted or used by the group you're selling to. Getting it out there is not enough, it has to make sense.

For example, if you run ads for your new brand of beer on the health and wellness TV station, your sales likely won't be as high as if you aired it during the evenings in between reality TV shows.

Top Secrets to Create A Top Performing Business

Marketing Collateral

This method is often confused with advertising, however it is self-promotion in the fact you don't use any other source to help you get your message across.

Below are commonly used examples:

- Business Cards
- Brochures
- Newsletters
- Flyers
- Posters

Public Relations

This is exposure to your company, and/or product/service that comes from a 3rd party – the media. To maintain the legitimacy of the information portrayed in this way you cannot pay for this exposure.

It comes instead by developing positive relationships with people within the media channels. When they understand your company vision, or product potential, you can work together to create communication to the public.

Top Secrets to Create A Top Performing Business

A good way to create a positive image of your company is to sponsor an event which gives back to the community. Then you would want to call up your buddy Jim at the local newspaper or Sally at your town's popular radio station, and chances are they'll help you promote it. It's a nice two way stream because as part of their job they are always looking for stories that will appeal to the public. And now here you are doing something that shows social awareness and involvement.

Traditional Sales

This method of promotion refers to yourself, a member of your sales team, or a retailer communicating about you product/services in a one to one or small group situation.

Examples include:

- Demonstrations/presentations
- Door-to-door
- Telemarketing

Sponsorship

This is a way to get exposure by affiliating yourself with another organization. You would offer financial support to this company's event, and in turn they would mention you when promoting their event.

You can use sponsorship in many ways. You can use it to create a positive image, by supporting an event that is important to everyone, e.g. Weekend to End Breast Cancer. Alternatively, it works well when you support a company whose product/service is related to you own, e.g. if you are a shoe company you could sponsor a local 10 km race.

Sales Promotion

Not to be confused with the word promotion itself; sales promotion is the action of offering incentives to entice people to try your product/service. These methods are often used to offer a "taster" of your product or service. They serve as a way of bringing in new clients, who you may not have reached without this bait.

It is also a way of attracting customers from your competitors; who may try your similar product/service because of the low rate, and then be "won over" by the quality of your product/service.

The idea is to make the consumers "an offer they can't refuse".

It is often used for a short time; but if long-term goals are set, and the sales promotion is well planned/ executed with them in mind, it can bring success on this level too.

Top Secrets to Create A Top Performing Business

Use sales promotion(s) in the short-term if you're looking to:

- Match the competition
- Move inventory
- Create cash flow

Use sales promotion(s) in the long-term if you're looking to:

- Create additional revenue or market share
- Increase the size of your target market
- Create a positive experience with the product/service
- Enhance product value and brand power

By this point I'm sure you're dying to know, what are these tools I can use to achieve such great things? Well they are things that we see every day when out in the marketplace. Examples:

1. Coupons – discounted prices are always appealing
2. Gift with purchase offers – to appeal to the "I get more than I'm paying for" mentality
3. Sweepstakes/Contests – you get a chance to win with every purchase
4. Free Samples – there's no risk involved, you know what you're buying

5. Specialties – free gifts used as a reminder items (carry your branding/logo)

6. Rebates – get money back if you mail in form

7. Group Discounts

8. Frequent User Incentives – e.g. Get your 7th coffee free after purchasing 6. This is a way to encourage customer loyalty

9. Give-Aways (e.g. Baseball caps or mugs with your logo) – now the public's doing your promoting for you

10. "Early Bird Rates" - this is useful if you are trying to get people to sign up for something, e.g. If you sign-up for this workshop before Oct. 14th the cost is $150.00, after that date it's $180

11. Guarantees – If you're not satisfied with your purchase you can return it for a refund

Packaging

Making sure that the container for your product is appealing, and that it offers the same message as the rest of your promotional efforts is essential. What good is going through all the planning to create a wonderful promotional campaign if a) when the customer gets the product or goes to buy it doesn't draw them in or b) they can't find it because the design fails (e.g. the company or product name is too small or gets lost behind lots of artsy filler).

Top Secrets to Create A Top Performing Business

Customer Service

Now let's say you don't have a product, but a service instead. Even if you are a small business you may have a few employees. It's important that all of the members of your team display a unite front, and communicate the promotion of your service in a consistent manner. And if what your company offers involves these employees providing it for the customer, it is especially important that there is a standard level of service. This is what helps build your brand.

Direct Mail

This involves sending out promotional materials addressed to specific individuals. This has become an increasingly popular method of promotion over the last five years.

There are even sources from whom you can buy databases of companies/individuals within your industry, allowing you to send your communication efforts to the people who are the most likely to need your product/services.

Personalizing the promotional materials you send out the response rates increases the "call to action" (specific result you're trying to achieve). The response rates are higher because people by nature are more inquisitive when they see something with their name on it, rather than what may just be perceived as a general flyer.

Trade Shows

Your product or service might be one that is suited to exhibiting at a trade show attended by your target audience. Trade shows are typically one- or two- day events that allow businesses to set up exhibits or booths showcasing their products or capabilities.

Choosing a Strategy

So with all these options, how do you decide which types of promotions will be the most effective, and will give you the most "bang for your buck"?

Keep these two things in mind:

Research is crucial. This means studying your target market; as well as the competition. Check out a trade magazine to see how they are marketing similar products/services.

A little creativity can go a long way. Think outside the box, and put your own spin on things. In such an environment that's saturated with so many marketing messages, doing something out of the ordinary will catch consumer attention, make you stand out and give you an edge on the competition.

Planning Your Promotions

Like anything in life, and especially in marketing; a well thought out plan is the starting point from which great successes arise. Just as it is necessary to write a general marketing plan; in order to assess your current situation, where you want to go and what it will look like when you get there; the same must be done to get a clear vision of what you want to achieve from your promotional efforts – your promotional campaign.

What is a promotional plan?

A promotional plan is an outline of the ways you're going to promote your product/service to achieve your marketing goals. The promotional plan is only one component of an overall marketing plan, yet it often gets mistaken however for the marketing plan, as it outlines where most of the marketing budget will go.

What do you want to achieve from your promotional efforts?

This is where you would discuss your goals. It is very important to remember that the goals of your promotional efforts are geared to achieve the goals that were set in your marketing plan. Just like the goals in the marketing plan need to focus on achieving the overall objectives of your company.

You want to be as specific as possible here. Just like you don't want to try and be everything to everyone - in terms of your product in the marketplace, you don't want to try and achieve every marketing goal you set at once. Really focus on what you're trying to achieve, whether it be results in the short-term, or paving the way for long-term success. Then just ensure that those are the marketing goals you're working from.

Remember that in order to know whether your efforts have been successful; you have to think in measurable terms from the goal setting phase. By comparing the following two goals it is clear to see which one will be more effective. Goal A = Increase of customers from implementing our new "return business rate". VS Goal B = Increased the repeat customer base by 20%, by year's end, as a result of the newly implemented "return business rate" program.

What message or image do you want to communicate?

You want to make sure that your customers are continually getting the same impression of your product/service, and your company as a whole. To ensure this happens as often as possible, you want to carefully choose what you want to convey.

Then, make sure all the forms of promotion you take lead back to these core communication messages. This is a similar concept to how your promotional efforts need to correspond with your marketing goals and your marketing goals need to correspond to your company goals.

In our environment we are continually surrounded by messages from different companies. They reach us on deeper levels than we realize. For this reason it is so important to maintain consistency in what and how you are communicating with your target market. The idea is that they get the same message so often that they don't even need to distinguish where or how they got it, it just becomes their association with what you are promoting.

This can only be achieved if you don't have conflicting messages. For example, if your packaging focuses on being environmentally friendly, your advertising campaign is about the great value for money of your product and your press releases discuss the health benefits the consumer is confused. What are you trying to provide me? All these different messages conflict in their minds and they are left felling confused, rather than compelled to buy/try your product.

What tools are you going to use to get your message across and achieve your goals?

The varieties of methods you can use to promote your product/services are limited only by your creativity.

What needs to be done for the plan to come into effect?

This is where you look at logistics. Things to think about:

- What kinds of companies will you need to research? (e.g. media, printing, design)
- When does the campaign need to be "up and running?"
- Will all your promotional efforts begin simultaneously, or will they be staggered?
- If you have staff, who will be responsible for what?

How much is it likely to cost to put these promotional efforts in place?

You need to consider how much your promotional vision will cost. And of course, going hand in hand with that is; how much do you have to spend?

One thing to keep in mind is whether or not the need for your product/service changes throughout the year. For example, if you sell snowshoes, this is a seasonal business, and you are not going to need to allot any of your budget toward promoting in the summer.

How will I know if I've achieved my goals? And how will I make sure to keep achieving them?

Having a maintenance plan for monitoring your promotional efforts is a key step; and should not to be overlooked. It ties into the idea of making sure that you're working toward measurable goals. If you don't have a specific result in mind, how do you know when/if you've achieved your goal?

Top Secrets to Create A Top Performing Business

Ways to discover which of your promotional efforts are most effective:

Customers: Your customers are the greatest source you have. After all, your efforts are aimed to appeal to them, so find out which of your promotional activities worked, by asking: "how did you hear about our product/service?" This is the best measure of success you could ask for...and it's free!

Retailers: If you are selling your product via someone else's store, make sure to connect with them regularly to see how things are going. They are an eye-witness to how your product fares against the competition. Find out what they notice in terms of customer perception of your product.

They will also be a different source of feedback than that which comes directly from the customer. They may be privy to information a customer wouldn't tell you, and will likely know all about the praise and/or complaints. So be sure to check in with questions such as: "have they noticed customers picking up your brochures or business cards you left at their store"?

Keep a notebook of comments, feedback and advice from these sources. By referring back to the info you have received by simply seeking this feedback; you can assess which promotional method is

146

bringing in the most sales, and then put more of your efforts and marketing budget toward it in the future.

Promotion Plan Steps

1. Go through the different types of promotional methods and determine their strengths and weaknesses

2. Determine the combination of promotion methods you want to implement

3. Decide which of the goals in your marketing plan you want to achieve with your promotional campaign

4. Look at how much money you have in the budget to allot to promotion

5. Decide what percentage of the budget will go to which method of promotion

6. Determine which messages (aspects) your company and its product/service you want to promote

7. Launch your promotional campaign when all the steps of planning (section D) have been completed

8. Evaluate the results of your promotional efforts

9

How to Create Repeat Business and Have Clients that Pay, Stay and Refer

When it comes to marketing and generating more income, most business owners are focused outward.

They've carefully established and segmented their target market, and created specific offers and messages for each market segment. They spend thousands of dollars in advertising and direct mail campaigns in hot pursuit of more leads, more customers, and more foot traffic.

While this is an effective way to build a business, it is costly and time consuming. It requires constant and consistent effort, and while this approach does generate results, those results quickly disappear when the effort stops or becomes less intense.

Successful businesses that see sustained growth have a double-edged marketing strategy. They focus their efforts *outward* – on new potential customers and marketing – as well as *inward* – on existing customers and referral business.

These successful businesses have leveraged their existing efforts to generate more revenue. Simply put, their customers buy from them over and over again.

For most businesses, this is the easiest way to increase their revenues. Simple customer loyalty strategies and outstanding customer service are often all you need to dramatically increase your sales – from the customers you already have.

The Cost of Your Customers

Do you know how much it costs your business to buy new customers?

Each new customer that walks through your door – with the exception of referrals – has cost you money to acquire. You have spent money on advertising and promotions to generate leads and turn those leads into customers.

For example, if you have placed an ad in your local newspaper for $1,000, and the ad brings in 10 customers, you have paid $100 to acquire each customer. You would need to ensure each of those customers spent at least $200 to cover your margin and break even.

Alternately, if you spent two hours of your time and $10 per month on an email marketing program to send a newsletter to your existing database of customers, and you bring in 10 customers as a result – each customer has cost you $1.

Generating more repeat business means focusing on the marketing strategies that aim to keep your existing customers instead of purchase new ones – effectively reducing the cost of attracting new customers to your business.

These strategies are simple to implement, and don't require much time investment. Just a solid understanding of how to make customers want to come back and spend more of their money

Keeping Your Customers

Marketing strategies that focus on keeping your current customer base are easy and enjoyable to implement. They allow you to build real relationships with the people you do business with, instead of dealing with a revolving door of people on the other end of your sales process.

Repeat customers create a community of people around your business that presumably share the same needs, desires and frustrations. The information you gain from these customers (market research) can help you strengthen your understanding of your target audience, and more accurately segment it.

Remember – 80% of your revenue comes from 20% of your customers. Always focus on these customers. They are ideal customers that you want to recruit, and hold on to.

Customer Service: Make them love buying from you

Every business – even those with excellent service standards can improve the service they provide their customers. Customer service seems to be a dying concept in most businesses; more focus seems to be placed on the speed of the transaction. These days you can even go to the grocery store now and not speak to a single sales associate thanks to self-serve checkouts.

To improve your company's customer service standards, take a survey of your customers and your employees to brainstorm ways you can improve the experience of buying from your business.

Successful customer service standards – those that make your customers *buy* – are:

Consistent. The standards are up kept by every person in your organization. Expectations are clear and followed through. Customers know what to expect, and choose your business because of those expectations.

Convenient. It is nearly effortless for the customer to spend money at your place of business. Convenience can take many forms – location, product selection, value-added services like delivery – and it is also consistent.

Customer-driven. The service the customer receives is exactly how they would like to be treated when buying your product or service. It is reflective of your target market, and appropriate to their lifestyle. Customers would probably not appreciate white linen tablecloths at a fast food restaurant, but they would appreciate a 2-minutes or less guarantee.

Newsletters: Keep in touch with your customers

A regular newsletter is an easy, time-effective, and inexpensive marketing strategy to implement. Unfortunately, many small businesses think these are too time consuming and too expensive to adopt as part of their marketing strategy.

The most popular type of newsletter distribution is email. This will cost your business as little at $10 per month for an email marketing service subscription, and can be customized to your unique branding.

Top Secrets to Create A Top Performing Business

Here is an easy five-step process to starting a company newsletter:

1. Pick your audience. New customers? Market segment? Existing customers?

2. Choose what you're going to say. Company news? Feature product? New offer?

3. Determine how you're going to say it. Articles? Bullet points? Pictures?

4. Decide how it's going to get to your audience. Email? Mail? In-store?

5. Track your results. How many people opened it? Read it? Took action?

Value Added Service: Give them happy surprises

Adding value to your business is an effective way of getting your customers back. Every person I know would choose a mattress store that offered free delivery over one that did not. It's that simple.

There are many ways to add value to your business, including:

o **Feature your expertise.** Use your knowledge to provide additional value to your customers. Offer a free consumer guide or report with every purchase.

153

o **Add convenience services.** Offer a service that makes their purchase easier, or more convenient. The best example of this is free shipping or delivery.

o **Package complementary services**. Packaging like items together creates an increase in perceived value. This is great for start-up kits.

o **Offer new products or services**. Feature top of the line or exclusive products, available only at your business. Offer a new service or profile a new staff member with niche expertise.

Value added services generate repeat customers in one of two ways:

1. Impress them on their first visit. Impress you customer with great service, a product that meets their needs, and then wow them with something extra that they weren't expecting. Get them to associate the experience of dealing with your business with happy surprises, and create a perception of higher value.

2. Entice them to come back. The introduction of a new value-added service can be enough to convince a customer to buy from you again. Their initial purchase established a trust and knowledge of your business and its processes. They will want to "be included" in anything new you have to offer – especially if there is exclusivity. It is easier to attract clients that have purchased from you than potential clients who have not.

Customer Loyalty Programs: Give them incentives

Another simple way to keep in touch with existing customers and keep them coming back to you is to create a customer loyalty program.

These programs do not have to be complicated or costly, and are relatively easy to maintain once they have been implemented. These programs help you gain more information on your customers and their purchasing habits.

Here are some examples of simple loyalty programs that you can implement:

Free product or service. Give them every 10th (or 6th) product or service free. Produce stamp cards with your logo and contact information on it.

Reward dollars. Give them a certain percentage of their purchase back in money that can only be spent in-store. Produce "funny money" with your logo and brand.

Top Secrets to Create A Top Performing Business

Rewards points. Give them a certain number of points for every dollar they spend. These points can be spent in-store, or on special items you bring in for points only.

Membership amenities. Give members access to VIP amenities that are not available to other customers. Produce member cards or give out member numbers.

Remember that in order for this strategy to work, you and your team have to understand and promote it. The program in itself becomes a product that you sell.

10

How to Double your Referrals

What if I told you that you could put an inexpensive system in place that would effectively allow your business to growth itself?

For most business owners, a large part of their customer base is comprised of referral customers. These people found out about the company's products or services from the recommendation of a friend or colleague who had a positive experience purchasing from that company.

If your business benefits from referral customers, you will find that these customers arrive ready to buy from you, and tend to buy more often. They also tend to be highly loyal to your product or service.

Seem like great customers to have, don't they?

Referral customers cost less to acquire. Compared to the leads you generate from advertising, direct mail campaigns, and other marketing initiatives, referral customers come to you already qualified and already trusting in the quality of your offering and the respectability of your staff.

With a little effort, and the creation of a formalized system – or strategy – you can not only continue to enjoy referral business, but easily double the number of referral customers that walk through your door. All of this is possible for a minimal investment of time and resources.

Is Your Business a Referral Business?

Referral based businesses benefit from a stream of qualified customers who arrive at their doorstep ready to spend. These businesses put less focus on advertising to generate new leads, and more focus on serving and communicating with their existing customers.

Generally speaking, a referral program can generate outstanding results for nearly any business. Since most referrals do not require any effort, the addition of a strategy and a program will often double or triple the number of qualified referrals that come through a business door.

There are, however, a few types of businesses that will not benefit from a formalized referral strategy. These are businesses with low price points – like fast food restaurants and drugstores. Their customer base is large already, and their efforts would be best spent on increasing the average sale.

A referral program can:

- **Save you time**. Referral strategies – once established – don't require much management or time investment.

- **Deliver more qualified customers**. Your customer arrives with an assumption of trust, and willing to purchase.

- **Improve your reputation.** Your customer's networks likely overlap, and create potential for a single customer to be referred by two people. This encourages the perception that your business is "the place to go."

- **Speed the sales process.** You will have existing common ground and a reputation with the referred customer.

- **Increase your profit.** You will spend less time and money generating leads, and more time serving customers who have their wallets open.

The Cost of Your Customers

As we discussed in the "Repeat Business" section, you don't "get" customers, you *buy* them. The money you spend on advertising, direct mail, and other promotions ideally results in potential customers walking through your doors.

For example, if you placed an ad for $200, and 20 people make a purchase in response to that ad, you would have paid $10 for each customer.

Referral customers cost you next to nothing. Your existing customer does the work of selling your business to their friend or associate, and you benefit from the sale. Aside from the cost of any referral incentives or coupon production, there is no cost involved at all.

Referral customers cost less and require less time investment than any other customer. That means you can spend that time making them a loyal customer, or a devoted fan.

Groom Your Customers

Referral strategies can allow you to groom your customer base. As we have previously discussed, 80% of your revenue comes from 20% of your customers – these are your ideal customers.

These are also the people you have established as your target market, and are the people you cater your marketing and advertising efforts toward.

You also have a group of customers who make up 80% of your headaches. These are the people who complain the most and spend the least.

Use your referral strategy to get more of your *ideal* customers. Spend more time servicing your ideal customers – do everything you can to make them happy – and less time on your headache customers. You can even ask your headache customers to shop elsewhere.

Then, focus your referral efforts on your ideal customers. Ask them to refer business to you, and reward them for doing so. Try to avoid referrals from your headache customers – chances are you'll just get another headache.

Referral Sources

Take some time to brainstorm all the people who could potentially refer business to you. Think beyond your business, to your extracurricular activities and personal life. There are endless sources of people who are ready and willing to send potential customers your way.

Here are some ideas to get you started:

Past Relationships

No, not romantic relationships. I'm talking about anyone you have previously had a relationship with, but for one reason or another have fallen out of touch. This includes former colleagues, associates, customers and friends.

Including them in your referral strategy can be as simple as reaching out through the phone or email, and updating them on your latest business initiative or career move. Gently ask at the end of the correspondence to refer anyone who may need your product or service. They will appreciate that you have attempted to re-establish the relationship.

Top Secrets to Create A Top Performing Business

Suppliers and Vendors

Your suppliers and vendors can be a great source for referrals, because they presumably deal daily with businesses that are complementary to your own. The opportunities to connect two of their customers in a mutually beneficial relationship are endless. These businesses should be happy to help out - especially if you have been a regular and loyal customer.

Customers

Customers are an obvious source of referrals because they are the people who are dealing with you directly on a regular basis. Often, all you have to do is ask and they will happily provide you with contact information of other interested buyers, or contact those buyers themselves.

Your customers also have a high level of product knowledge when it comes to your business, and are in a great position to really sell the strength of your company. Remember from the Testimonials section, the words of your customers are at least 10 times more powerful than any clever headline or marketing piece you could create.

Top Secrets to Create A Top Performing Business

Employees and Associates

Give your employees and associates a reason to have their friends and families shop at your business with a simple incentive program. These people have the most product knowledge, and are in the best position to sell you to a potential customer.

This is also a way to tap into an endless network of people. Who do your employees and associates know? Who do their friends and friends of friends know? A referral chain that connects to your employees can be a highly powerful one.

Competitors

This doesn't seem so obvious, but it can work. Your direct competitors are clearly not the ideal source for referrals. However, indirect competitors can refer their clients or potential clients to you if they cannot meet those clients' needs themselves.

For example, if you sell high end lighting fixtures, the low-budget lighting store down the street may be able to refer clients to you, and vice versa. You may wish to offer a finder's fee or incentive to establish this arrangement.

Top Secrets to Create A Top Performing Business

Your Network

Don't be shy about asking your friends and family members for referrals. Too many people do not provide enough information to their inner circle about what they do or what their business does. This doesn't make sense, since these are the people who should be the most interested!

Take time to explain clearly what your business is all about, and what your point of difference is. Then just ask them if they know anyone who may benefit from what you are offering. You could even provide your friends and family with an incentive – a gift, a meal, or a portion of the sale.

Associations + Special Interest Groups

This is another place you likely have a network of people who have limited knowledge about what you do or what your business does. The advantage here is that you have a group of people with similar belief s and values in the same room. Use it!

Top Secrets to Create A Top Performing Business

The Media

Unless a member of the media is a regular customer of yours, or you are in business to serve the media, this may not seem like an obvious choice either.

The opportunity here is to establish a relationship with an editor or journalist, and position yourself as an expert in your field or industry. Then, next time they are writing a related story, they can ask to quote you and your opinion. When their audience reads the story, they will perceive your business as the industry leader.

Referral Strategies

A referral strategy is any system you can put in place to generate new leads through existing customers. The ideal way to do this is to create a system that runs itself! Here are some ideas for simple strategies you can begin to implement into your business immediately.

Just Ask

This may seem simple and obvious, but it's true. Be open with your customers and associates, and simply ask them if they can refer any of their friends or associates to you. Make it part of doing business with you, and your customers will grow to expect the question. Or, let them know in advance that you'll be asking at a later date.

Remember that this can include potential customers – even if they don't buy from you. The reason they chose not to purchase may have nothing to do with your business; any person who has begun to or actually done business with you can refer to you another person.

Offer Incentives

When you speak to your customers, when you ask them for something, you typically try to answer the question "what's in it for me?" before they ask it.

The same is true when you ask your customers for a referral. Incentive-based referral strategies work wonders, and can easily be implemented as part of a customer loyalty program, or as part of your existing customer relations systems.

Consider offering customers who successfully refer clients to you discounts on products, free products or services, or gifts. Offer incentives relative to the number of referrals, or the success rate of each referral.

Top Secrets to Create A Top Performing Business

This can have a spin off effect, as your referral customers may become motivated to continue the referral chain. They too will be interested in the incentives you have provided, and tell their friends about your business.

Be Proactive

The only way your referral program will work is if you put some effort into it, and maintain some level of ongoing effort.

Here are some ideas:

- Put a referral card or coupon in every shopping bag that leaves your store
- Promote gift certificates during peak seasons
- Offer free information seminars to existing customers, and ask them to bring a friend
- Host a closed-door sale for your top 20 customers and their friends

Provide Great Customer Service

An easy way to encourage referral business is to treat every potential customer with exemplary customer service. Since the art of customer service is lost is many communities, people are often impressed by simple added touches and conveniences. That alone will encourage them to refer your business to their network.

Stay in Touch

Make sure you are staying in touch with all of your potential and converted customers. Through newsletters, direct mail, or the Internet, keep your business name at the top of the minds, ahead of the competition.

Even if they have already purchased from you, and may not need to purchase for some time, a newsletter or email can be a simple reminder that your business is out there. If someone in their network is looking for the product or service, it will be more likely that your customer will refer your business over the competition.

11

Immediate Sales

If you're a business owner, you're also a salesperson.

You've had to sell the bank to get them to loan you your start-up capital. You've had to sell the best employees on why they should work for your business. You've had to convince your business partner, spouse, and friends why your business idea is a good one.

Now you have to repeatedly sell your product or service to your customers.

The ability to sell effectively and efficiently is one every successful business owner has cultivated, and continues to develop. It can be a complicated and time consuming task; one that you will have to continually work on throughout your career in order to be – and stay – successful.

Fortunately, making sales is a step-by-step process that can be learned, customized, and continuously improved. There are a wide range of tools available to help and support your sales efforts.

You don't have to be the most outgoing, enthusiastic person to be successful at sales. You don't even have to be a good public speaker. All you need is an understanding of the basic sales process, and a genuine passion for what you are selling.

Sales 101

As I said before, making sales is a process. There are clear, step-by-step actions that can be taken and result in a sale.

The sales process varies according to the type of business, type of customers and type of product or service that is offered; however, the core steps are the same. Similarly, sales training varies from individual to individual, but the core skills and abilities remain the same.

Here is a basic seven-step process that you can follow, or fine tune to suit your unique products and services. Remember that each step is important, and builds on the step previous. It is essential to become adept at each step, instead of solely focusing on closing the sale.

Top Secrets to Create A Top Performing Business

1. Preparation

Make sure you have prepared for your meeting, presentation, or day on the sales floor. You have complete control of this part of the sales process, so it is important to do everything you can to set the stage for your success.

- Understand your product or service inside and out.
- Prepare all the necessary materials, and organize them neatly.
- Keep your place of business tidy and organized. Reface product on shelves.
- Ensure you appear professional and well groomed.
- Do some research on your potential client and brainstorm to find common ground.

2. Build a Relationship

The first few minutes you spend with a potential customer set the stage for the rest of your interaction. First impressions are everything. Your goal in the second step is to relax the customer and begin to develop a relationship with them. Establishing a real relationship with your customer will create trust.

- Make a great first impression: shake hands, make eye contact, and introduce yourself.
- Remain confident and professional, but also personable.
- Mirror their speech and behavior.
- Begin with general questions and small talk.
- Show interest in them and their place of business.
- Notice and comment on positives.
- Find some common ground on which to relate.

3. Discuss Needs + Wants

Once you have spent a few moments getting to know your prospect, start asking open-ended questions to discover some of their needs and wants. If they have come to you on the sales floor, ask what brought them in the store. If you are meeting them to present your product or service, ask why they are interested in, or what criteria they have in mind for that product or service.

- If you are making a sales presentation, ask for a few moments at the outset to outline the purpose of your visit, as well as how you have structured the presentation.
- Listen intently, and repeat back information you are not sure you understand.

- Ask open-ended questions to get them talking. The longer they talk, the more insight they are providing you into their needs and purchase motivations.
- Ask clarifying questions about their responses.
- If you become sure the customer is going to buy your product or service, begin to ask questions specific to the offering. i.e., what size/color do you prefer?

4. Present the Solution

Once you have a solid understanding of what they are looking for, or what issue they are looking to resolve, you can begin to present the solution: your product or service.

- Explain how your product or service will solve their problem or meeting their needs. If several products apply, begin by presenting the mid-level product.
- Illustrate your points with anecdotes about other happy customers, or awards the product or service has earned.
- Use hypothetical examples featuring your customer. Encourage them to picture a scenario after their purchase.
- Begin by describing the benefits of the product, then follow up with features and advantages.

- Watch your customer's behavior as you speak, and ask further qualifying questions in response to body language and verbal comments.
- Give the customer an opportunity to ask you questions or provide feedback about each product or service after you have described or explained it.
- Ask closed-ended questions to gain agreement.

5. Overcome Objections

As you present the product or service, take note of potential objections by asking open-ended questions and monitoring body language. Expect that objections will arise and prepare for it. Consider brainstorming a list of all potential objections, and writing down your responses.

- Repeat the objection back to the customer to ensure you understand them correctly.
- Empathize with what they have said, and then provide a response that overcomes the objection.
- Confirm that the answer you have provided has overcome their objection by repeating yourself.

The Eight Most Common Objections

The product or service does not seem valuable to me.
There is no reason for me to act know. I will wait.
It's safest not to make a decision right away.
There is not enough money for the purchase.
The competitor or another department offers a better product.
There are internal issues between people or departments.
The relationship with the decision maker is strained.
There is an existing contract in place with another business.

---

6. Close

This is an important part of the sales process that should be handled delicately. Deciding when to close is a judgment call that must be made in the moment during the sale. Ideally, you have presented a solution to their problem, overcome objections, and have the customer in a place where they are ready to buy.

Here are some questions to ask before you close the sale:

- Does my prospect agree that there is value in my product or service?
- Does my prospect understand the features and benefits of the product or service?
- Are there any remaining objections that must be handled?

- What other factors could influence my prospect's decision to buy?
- Have I minimized the risk involved in the purchase, and provided some level of urgency?

Once you have determined it is time to make the sale, here are some sample statements you can use to get the process rolling:

- So, should we get started?
- Shall I grab a new one from the back?
- If you just give me your credit card, I can take care of the transaction while you continue browsing.
- When would you like the product delivered?
- We can begin next month if we receive payment by the end of the week.
- Can I email you a draft contract tomorrow?

7. Service + Follow-up

Once you have made the sale, your work is not over. You want to ensure that that customer will become a loyal, repeat customer, and that they will refer their friends to your business.

Ask them to be in your customer database, and keep in touch with regular newsletters. Follow up with a phone call or drop by to ask how they are enjoying the product or service, and if they have any further questions or needs you can assist them with.

This contact opportunity will also allow you ask for a referral, or an up sell. At the very least, it will ensure you are continuing to foster and build a relationship with the client.

Up selling

Up selling is simply inviting your customers to spend more money in your business by purchasing additional products or services. This could include more of the same product, complementary products, or impulse items.

Regardless, up selling is an effective way to increase profits and create loyal clients – without spending any money to acquire the business. These clients are already purchasing from you – which means they perceive value in what you have to offer – so take the information you have gained in the sales process and offer them a little bit more.

You experience up selling on a daily basis. From "do you want fries with that?" to "have you heard about our product protect program?" companies across the globe have tapped into and trained their staff on the value of the up sell.

Up selling is truly rooted in good customer service. If your client purchases a new computer printer, you'll need to make sure they have the cords required to connect it to the computer, regular and photo paper, and color and black and white ink.

If you don't suggest these items, they may arrive home and realize they do not have all the materials needed to use the product. They may choose to purchase those materials somewhere closer, cheaper, or more helpful.

Customer education is another form of up selling. What if you customer doesn't realize that you sell a variety of printer paper and stationery in addition to computer hardware like printers? Take every opportunity to educate your customer on the products and services you offer that may be of interest to them.

An effective way of implementing an up sell system into your business is simply by creating add-on checklists for the products or services you offer. Each item has a list of related items that your customer may need. This will encourage your staff to develop the habit of asking for the up sell.

Other up sell strategies can be implemented:

- **At the point of sale**. This is a great place for impulse items like candy, flashlights, nail scissors, etc.

- **In a newsletter**. This is an effective strategy for customer education.

- **In your merchandising**. Place strips of impulse items near related items. For example, paper clips with paper and pens near binders.

- **Over the phone**. If someone is placing an order for delivery, offer additional items in the same shipment for convenience.

- **With new products**. Feature each new product or service that you offer prominently in your business, and ask your staff to mention it to every customer.

Sales Team

Employing a team of strong salespeople

What Makes a Good Salesperson?

There are a lot of salespeople out there – but what qualities and skills make a great salesperson? These are the attributes you will want to find or develop in your team:

- Willingness to continuously learn and improve sales skills
- Sincerity in relating to customers and providing solutions to their objectives
- An understanding of the company's big picture
- A communication style that is direct, polite, and professional
- Honesty and respect for other team members, customers, as well as the competition.
- Ability to manage time
- Enthusiastic
- Inquisitive
- A great listener
- Ability to quickly interpret, analyze, and respond to information during the sales process
- Ability to connect and develop relationships of trust with potential clients
- Professional appearance

Team Building – Keeping Your Team Together

In many businesses, sales is a department or a whole team of people who work together to generate leads and convert customers. Effective management of your sales team is a skill every business owner should cultivate.

Teambuilding, recruitment, and training will be discussed in later sections, but take some time to consider the following aspects of managing a sales team:

Communication
- Are targets and results regularly reviewed?
- Are opportunities for input regularly provided?
- Do sales staff members have a clear understanding of what is expected?
- Do all staff members know daily, weekly, and quarterly targets?

Performance Management
- Are sales staff members motivated to reach targets?
- Are sales staff recognized and rewarded once those targets are reached?
- Are there opportunities for skills training and development?

- Do staff members have broad and comprehensive product or industry knowledge?
- Is there opportunity for growth within the company?
- Is performance regularly reviewed?

Operations

- Do you have a solid understanding of your sales numbers (revenue, profit, margins)?
- Are your sales processes regularly reviewed?
- Do you have a variety of sales scripts prepared?
- Do you measure conversion rates?
- How are your leads generated?

Sales Tools

Every salesperson should have an arsenal of tools on hand to assist them in the sales process. These tools can act as aids while a sale is taking place, or help to foster continual learning and development of the salesperson's skills and approach.

The list below includes some popular sales tools. Add to this list with other resources that are specific to your business or industry.

Top Secrets to Create A Top Performing Business

Tool	Description + Benefit
Scripts	Used for incoming and outgoing telemarketing, cold calls, door-to-door sales, in-store sales Create several different scripts throughout your business Maintains consistency in your sales approach Revise and renew your scripts regularly
Presentation Materials	High-quality information about your product or service Forms: PowerPoint presentation, brochure, product sheets, proposal Serves as an outline of your sales presentation, and keeps you on task
Colleagues	A source of help and advice, especially when you are on the same team or sell similar products Also a source of support
Customer Databases	An accurate, up-to-date database of customer contact information and contact history Used to stay in touch with clients Can also be used for direct mail and follow-up telemarketing
The Internet	A powerful resource for sales help and advice Information to help improve your sales process Online sales coaching Source for product knowledge
Ongoing Training	Constant improvement of your sales skills Constant increase in product knowledge Investment in yourself and your company

8 Tips for Better Sales

- **Dress for the sale.** Dress professionally, appear well put together and maintain good hygiene. Ensure you are not only dressed professionally, but *appropriately*. Would your client feel more comfortable if you wore a suit, or jeans and blazer?

- **Speak their language.** Show you understand their industry or culture, and use phrases your customer understands. This may require researching industry jargon or common phrases. Remember to avoid using words and phrases that are used in the sales process: sold, contract, telemarketing, finance, interest, etc. Doing so will help break down the salesperson/customer barrier.

- **Ooze positivity**. Show up or answer the phone with a smile, and leave your personal or business issues behind. Be enthusiastic about what you have to offer, and how that offering will benefit your customer. Reflect this not only in your voice, but also in your body language.

- **Deliver a strong pitch or presentation**. Be confident and convincing. Leave self-doubt at the door, and walk in assuming the sale. Take time to explain complex concepts, and always connect what you're saying to your audience in a specific way.

- **Be a poster-child for good manners**. Accept any amenity you're offered, listen intently, don't interrupt, don't show up late, have a strong handshake, and give everyone you are speaking to equal attention.

- **Avoid sensitive subjects**. Politics, religion, swearing, sexual innuendos and racial comments are absolutely off-limits. So are negative comments about other customers or the competition.

- **Create a real relationship.** Icebreakers and small talk are not just to pass the time before your presentation. They are how relationships get established. Show genuine interest in everything your customer has to say. Ask questions about topics you know they are passionate. Speak person to person, not salesperson to customer. Remember everything.

- **Know more than you need to.** Impress clients with comprehensive knowledge – not only of your product or service – but also of the people who use that product or service, and industry trends. Been seen as an expert in order to build trust and respect.

12

Creating a Powerful Offer

I'm not going to beat around the bush on this one:

Your offer is the granite foundation of your marketing campaign.

Get it right, and everything else will fall into place. Your headline will grab readers, your copy will sing, your ad layout will hardly matter, and you will have customers running to your door.

Get it wrong, and even the best looking, best-written campaign will sink like the Titanic.

A powerful offer is an irresistible offer. It's an offer that gets your audience frothing at the mouth and clamoring over each other all the way to your door. An offer that makes your readers pick up the phone and open their wallets.

Irresistible offers make your potential customers think, "I'd be crazy not to take him up on that," or "An offer like this doesn't come around very often." They instill a sense of emotion, of desire, and ultimately, urgency.

Make it easy for customers to purchase from you the first time, and spend your time keeping them coming back.

I'll say it again: **get it right, and everything else will fall into place.**

The Crux of Your Marketing Campaign

As you work your way through this program, you will find that nearly every chapter discusses the importance of a powerful offer as related to your marketing strategy or promotional campaign.

There's a reason for this. The powerful offer is more often than not the reason a customer will open their wallets. It is how you generate leads, and then convert them into loyal customers. The more dramatic, unbelievable, and valuable the offer is the more dramatic and unbelievable the response will be.

Many companies spend thousands of dollars on impressive marketing campaigns in glossy magazines and big city newspapers.

They send massive direct mail campaigns on a regular basis; yet don't receive an impressive or massive response rate.

These companies do not yet understand that simply providing information on their company and the benefits of their product is not enough to get customers to act. There is no reason to pick up the phone or visit the store, *right now*.

Your powerful, irresistible offer can:
- Increase leads
- Drive traffic to your website or business
- Move old product
- Convert leads into customers
- Build your customer database

What Makes a Powerful Offer?

A powerful offer is one that makes the most people respond, and take action. It gets people running to spend money on your product or service.

Powerful offers nearly always have an element of *urgency* and of *scarcity*. They give your audience a reason to act immediately, instead of put it off until a later date.

Top Secrets to Create A Top Performing Business

Urgency relates to time. The offer is only available until a certain date, during a certain period of the day, or if you act within a few hours of seeing the ad. The customer needs to act now to take advantage of the offer.

Scarcity related to quantity. There are only a certain number of customers who will be able to take advantage of the offer. There may be a limited number of spaces, a limited number of products, or simply a limited number of people the business will provide the offer to. Again, this requires that customer acts immediately to reap the high value for low cost.

Powerful offers also:

Offer great value. Customers perceive the offer as having great value – more than a single product on its own, or the product at its regular price. It is clear that the offer takes the reader's needs and wants into consideration.

Make sense to the reader. They are simple and easy to understand if read quickly. Avoid percentages – use half off or 2 for 1 instead of 50% off. There are no "catches" or requirements; no fine print.

Seem logical. The offer doesn't come out of thin air. There is a logical reason behind it – a holiday, end of season, anniversary celebration, or new product. People can get suspicious of offers that seem "too good to be true" and have no apparent purpose.

Provide a premium. The offer provides something extra to the customer, like a free gift, or free product or service. They feel they are getting something extra for no extra cost. Premiums are perceived to have more value than discounts.

Remember that when your target market reads your offer, they will be asking the following questions:

1. What are you offering me?
2. What's in it for me?
3. What makes me sure I can believe you?
4. How much do I have to pay for it?

The Most Powerful Types of Offers

Decide what kind of offer will most effectively achieve your objectives. Are you trying to generate leads, convert customers, build a database, move old product off the shelves, or increase sales?

Consider what type of offer will be of most value to your ideal customers – what offer will make them act quickly.

Top Secrets to Create A Top Performing Business

Free Offer

This type of offer asks customers to act immediately in exchange for something free. This is a good strategy to use to build a customer database or mailing list. Offer a free consultation, free consumer report, or other item of low cost to you but of high perceived value.

You can also advertise the value of the item you are offering for free. For example, act now and you'll receive a free consultation, worth $75 dollars. This will dramatically increase your lead generation, and allow you to focus on conversion when the customer comes through the door or picks up the phone.

The Value Added Offer

Add additional services or products that cost you very little, and combine them with other items to increase their attractiveness. This increases the perception of value in the customer's mind, which will justify increasing the price of a product or service without incurring extra hard costs to your business.

Package Offer

Package your products or services together in a logical way to increase the perceived value as a whole. Discount the value of the package by a small margin, and position it as a "start-up kit" or "special package." By packaging goods of mixed values, you will be able to close more high-value sales. For example: including a free desk-jet printer with every computer purchase.

Premium Offer

Offer a bonus product or service with the purchase of another. This strategy will serve your bottom line much better than discounting. This includes 2 for 1 offers, offers that include free gifts, and in-store credit with purchases over a specific dollar amount.

Urgency Offer

As I mentioned above, offers that include an element of urgency enjoy a better response rate, as there is a reason for your customers to act immediately. Give the offer a deadline or limit the number of spots available.

Guarantee Offer

Offer to take the risk of making a purchase away from your customers. Guarantee the performance or results of your product or service, and offer to compensate the customer with their money back if they are not satisfied. This will help overcome any fear or reservations about your product, and make it more likely for your leads to become customers.

Create Your Powerful Offer

1. Pick a single product or service.

Focus on only one product or service – or one product or service *type* – at a time. This will keep your offer clear, simple, and easy to understand. This can be an area of your business you wish to grow, or old product that you need to move off the shelves.

2. Decide what you want your customers to do.

What are you looking to achieve from your offer? If it is to generate more leads, then you'll need your customer to contact you. If it is to quickly sell old product, you'll need your customer to come into the store and buy it. Do you want them to visit your website? Sign up for your newsletter? How long do they have to act? Be clear about your call to action, and state it clearly in your offer.

3. Dream up the biggest, best offer.

First, think of the biggest, best things you could offer your customers – regardless of cost and ability. Don't limit yourself to a single type of offer, combine several types of offers to increase value. Offer a premium, plus a guarantee, with a package offer. Then take a look at what you've created, and make the necessary changes so it is realistic.

4. Run the numbers.

Finally, make sure the offer will leave you with some profit – or at least allow you to break even. You don't want to publish an outrageous offer that will generate a tremendous number of leads, but leave you broke. Remember that each customer has an acquisition cost, as well as a lifetime value. The amount of their first purchase may allow you to break even, but the amount of their subsequent purchases may make you a lovely profit.

13

Use Scripts to Increase Sales Immediately

What do playbooks, prompts, guides and scripts all have in common?

They are all popular tools that dictate or guide human behavior toward a desired outcome.

Playbooks help coaches tell sports teams specifically how to play the game to overcome an opponent. Prompts help to kick-start writers and other creative professionals when stuck in a rut. Guides provide a series of instructions so that a person or team of people can complete or implement a specific task. Film scripts tell actors how to act for a particular part.

If you're in the business of sales, you also know about sales scripts. Sales scripts are tools that guide salespeople during interactions or conversations with potential customers.

A large number of businesses use scripts, either as a way of maintaining consistency amongst a sales team, training new salespeople, or enhancing their sales skills. They may have a single script, or several, and may change their scripts regularly, or use the same one for years.

.

What most businesses overlook, however, is that the sales script is a living, breathing, changing member of their sales team. They may be internal documents, but they deserve just as much time and effort as your marketing collateral.

Do You Really Need a Script?

The short answer is yes. You absolutely need a script for any and every customer interaction you and your salespeople may find yourselves in.

Sure, countless business owners and salespeople work every day without a script. If you own your own business, chances are you're already a pretty good salesperson. But if you are not using scripts, you're only working at half of your true potential – or half of your potential earnings.

Scripts don't have to be "cheesy" or read verbatim. They act as a map for your sales process, and provide prompts to trigger your memory and keep you on track. How many times have you made a cold call that didn't work out the way you wanted it to? Scripts dramatically improve the effectiveness and efficiency of your sales processes.

A comprehensive set of scripts will also keep a level of consistency amongst your salespeople and the customer service they provide your clients.

Once scripts are written, memorized, and rehearsed, they become like film scripts; the salesperson can breathe their own life and personality into the conversation, while staying focused on the call's objectives.

Why Your Scripts Aren't Working

If you a currently using scripts in your business, are they working? Are they as effective as they could possibly be? How do you know? When was the last time they were reviewed or updated?

Scripts are like any other element of your marketing campaign – they need to be tested and measured for results, and changed based on what is or is not working.

Measure the success of your script based on your conversion rates. Of all the people you speak to and use the script, how many are being converted from leads to sales?

When evaluating your existing scripts, ask yourself the following questions:

How old is this script? What was it written for? Scripts are living, breathing members of your company. They need to be written and rewritten and rewritten again as the needs of your customers change, your product or services change, or as new strategies are implemented.

Does this script address all the customer objections we regularly hear? Every time you hear a customer raise an objection that is not included on the script, add it. The power of your script lies in the ability to anticipate customer concerns, and answer them before they're raised.

Does this script sound the same as the others? Your scripts are part of the package that represents you as a company. There should be a consistent feel or approach throughout your scripts that your customers will recognize and feel confident dealing with.

Is everyone using the script? Who on your team regularly uses these scripts? Just the junior staff? Only the top-performing staff? Make sure everyone is singing from the same song sheet – your customers will appreciate the consistency.

Types of Scripts

Depending on the product or service you offer and the marketing strategies you have chosen, there are countless types of scripts you could potentially prepare for your business,

When you sit down to create your scripts, it would be wise to start by making a list of all the instances you and your staff members interact with your existing or potential customers. Then, prioritize the list from most to least important, and start writing from the top.

Here are some commonly used scripts, and their purposes:

Sales presentation script

Each time you or your sales staff make a presentation, they should be using the same or a slightly modified version of the same script. This script will include sample icebreakers, a presentation on benefits and features of the product or service, and a list of possible objections and responses. These scripts should also help alleviate some of the nervousness or anxiety associated with public speaking.

Closing script

Closing scripts help you do just that: close the sale. This could include a list of closing prompts or statements to get the transaction started. This type of script also includes a list of possible customer objections, and planned responses.

Incoming phone call script

Everyone who calls your business should be treated the same way; consistent information should be gathered and provided to the customer. The person answering the phone should state the company name, department name, and their own name in the initial greeting. This goes for both the main line, and each individual or department extension.

Cold call script

This is one of the most important scripts you can perfect for your business. The cold call script must master the art of quickly getting the attention of the customer, then engaging and persuading them with the benefits of the product or service. The caller needs to establish common ground with the potential customer, and find a way to get them talking through open-ended questions.

Direct mail follow-up script

Scripts for outgoing calls that are intended to follow up on a direct mail piece are essential for every direct mail campaign. They are designed to call qualified leads that have already received information and an offer, and convert them into customers. These scripts should focus on enticing customers to act, and overcoming any objections that may have prevented them from acting sooner.

Market research script

Scripts that are used primarily for the purpose of gathering information should be designed to get the customer talking. A focus on open-ended questions and relationship building statements will help to relax the customer, and encourage honest dialogue.

Difficult customer script

Just like every salesperson needs to practice the sales process, you and your staff also need to practice your ability to handle difficult customers. If you operate a retail business this is especially important, as difficult customers often present themselves in front of other customers. These scripts should help you diffuse the situation, calm the customer down, and then handle their objections.

Creating Scripts

Creating powerful scripts is not a complicated exercise, but it will take some time to complete. Focus on the most vital scripts for your business first, and engage the assistance of your sales staff in drafting or reviewing the scripts.

Your Script Binder

Keep master copies of all of your scripts in one organized place. An effective way to do this is to create a binder, and use tabs to separate each type of script.

You will also want to create a separate tab for customer objections, and list every single customer objection you have ever heard in relation to your product or service. Find a way to organize each objection so you can easily find them – group them by category or separate them with tabs.

Then, list your responses next to each objection – there should be several responses to each objection created with different customer types in mind. A master list of customer objections and responses is an invaluable tool for any business owner, salesperson, and script writer. The more responses you can think of, the better.

Remember, the script binder is never "finished." You will need to make sure that it is updated and added to on a regular basis.

Writing Scripts – Step by Step

Step One: Record What You're Doing Now

If you aren't using scripts – or even if you are – start by recording yourself in action. Use video or audio recording to tape yourself on the phone, in a sales presentation, or with a customer.

Make notes on your body language, word choice, customer reaction and body language, responses to objections, and closing statements.

You may also wish to ask an associate to make notes on your performance and discuss them with you in a constructive fashion.

Step Two: Evaluate What You're Doing Wrong

Take a look at your notes, and ask yourself the following questions:

- How are you engaging the customer?
- Are you building common ground and trust?
- Does what you are saying matter to the customer?
- Is your offer a powerful one?
- What objections are raised?
- How are you dealing with them?
- What objections are you avoiding?
- How natural is your close?
- Are you as effective as you think you can be?

Once you have answered and made notes in response to these questions, make a list of things you need to improve, and how you think you might go about doing so. Do you need to strengthen your closing statements? Do you need to brainstorm more responses to objections? Remember that everyone's script and sales process can be improved.

Step Three: Decide Who the Script is For

So now that you know the elements of your script you need to work on, you can begin drafting your new script, or revising an old one.

The first part of writing a script – or any piece of marketing material – is having a strong understanding of who you are writing it for. Who is your target audience? What does your ideal customer look like? Consider demographic characteristics like age, sex, location, income, occupation and marital status. Be as specific as possible. What are their purchase patterns? What motivates them to spend money?

If you are writing a cold call script, you will need to develop or purchase a list of people who fall into the target market specifics you have established. If you are writing a sales script for in-store customers, then spend some time reviewing what types of customers find their way into your place of business.

You will want to use words that your target audience will not only understand, but relate to and resonate with. Use sensory language that will trigger emotional and feeling responses – *I need this, this will solve that problem, I'll feel better if I have this, etc.*

Step Four: Decide What You Want to Say

There are typically five sections of every script – and there may be more, depending on the type and purpose of script:

Top Secrets to Create A Top Performing Business

1. Engage

- Get their attention or pique their interest
- Establish common ground
- Build trust, be human
- Ask for their time

2. Ask + Qualify

- Take control of the conversation by asking questions
- Focus on open-ended questions that cannot be answered with a "yes" or "no"
- Get the customer talking
- Ask as many questions as you need to get information on the customer's needs and purchase motivations

3. Get Agreement

- Ask closed-ended questions you are sure they will respond with "yes"
- Get them to agree on the benefits of the product or service
- Repeat key points back to the customer to gain agreement

4. Overcome Objections

- Anticipate objections based on customer comments, then refute them
- Make informative assumptions about their thought process, identify with their concern, then refute it using your own experiences
- Repeat concerns back to the customer to let them know you have heard them
- Ask about any remaining objections before you close

5. Close

- Assume that you have overcome all objections, and have the sale
- Ask the customer transactional questions, like delivery timing and payment method
- Be as confident and natural as possible

Step Five: Train Your Staff

Once you have written your company's scripts, you will need to ensure your staff understand and are comfortable using them.

Consider having a team meeting, and use role play to review each of the scripts. This will encourage your salespeople to practice amongst each other, and strengthen their sales skills. Ask them for feedback on the scripts, and make any necessary changes.

You will also need to decide how comfortable you are having your salespeople personalizing the scripts to suit their own styles. Be clear what elements of the script are "company standards" and essential techniques, but also be flexible with your team.

Step Six: Continually Revise

After you have carefully crafted your script, put it to the test. Practice on your colleagues, friends, and family. Get their feedback, and make changes.

Remember that scripts will need to change and evolve as your business changes and evolves, and new products or services are introduced. Keep your script binder on your desk at all times, and continually make changes and improvements to it.

You may also wish to record and evaluate your performance on a regular basis. This is an exercise you could incorporate into regular employee reviews, to use as a constructive tool for staff development.

Script Tips

- Practice anticipating and eliciting real objections – including the ones your customer doesn't want to raise.

- Make the script yours – it should look, feel, and sound like you naturally do, not like you're reading off the page.

- Spend time with the masters. If there is a salesperson you admire in your community, ask to observe them in action. Take notes on their performance, and the techniques they use for success.

- If your script is not successful, ask the customer why not? Even if you don't get the sale, you'll get a new objection you can craft responses to and never get stumped by it again.

- Don't fear objections. Just spend time identifying as many as possible, then practice overcoming them.

- Never stop thinking of responses to customer objections. Each objection could potentially have 30 responses, geared toward specific customer types.

- Anecdotes are persuasive writing tools – use them in your scripts. People enjoy hearing stories, especially stories that relate to them and their experiences, frustrations, and troubles. Let the story sell your product or service for you.

- Include body language in your scripts – it's just as important as your words. Try mimicking your subject's posture, arm position, and seating position. This is proven to create ease and build trust.

- If you only have your voice, use it. Pay attention to tone, language choice, speed, and background noise. You only have sound to establish a trusting relationships, so do it carefully.

- Be confident, and focus on a positive stream of self-talk to prepare for the call or presentation. Confidence sells.

- Spend time on your closing scripts, as they are a critical component of your presentation or phone call. This can be a challenging part of the sales process, so practice, practice, practice.

14

Create Added Value in Your Business and Make 1 + 1 = 3

The majority of small businesses, like yours, are established in response to market demand for a product or service. Many build their businesses by serving that demand, and enjoy growing profits without putting much effort into long-term planning or marketing.

However, what happens when that demand slows or stops? What happens when the competition sets up shop with a "new and improved" version of your product down the road? How do you keep your offering fresh, while growing and maintaining your client base? The answer is by adding value to your product or service.

Added value is a marketing or customer relations strategy that can take the form of a product, service, which is added to the original offering for free, or as part of a discounted package. It, like all other elements in your marketing toolkit, is designed to attract new customers and retain existing ones. A simple example of added value would be if you owned a gift shop, and offered complimentary gift wrapping with every purchase.

If you don't refresh and renew your offering over time, your customers will get bored and be drawn to your competitor. Your employees, too, may become disinterested, and find work elsewhere. Ultimately, both clients and employees will demand additional value to remain loyal – and aren't they the keystones for your business growth?

Can You Add Value to Your Business?

Everyone can add value to their business. Better yet, everyone can *afford* to add value to their business. Adding value doesn't have to blow your marketing budget, or take up hours of your time. There are many ways – big and small – to enhance your business in the eyes of your clients.

The key to adding value is determining what your customers and target market perceive as valuable. You must understand their needs, wants, troubles and inconveniences in order to entice them with solutions through added value products or services. Adding value will add to your profits, but if you don't focus on genuinely helping your clients, you'll have a difficult time attracting them.

Added value works for both product- and service-based businesses. If you offer a service, like hairstyling, try treating your customers with products like a latte while they wait, shampoo samples, or a free conditioning treatment with every sixth visit. If you sell a product, consider offering convenience services – like free shipping or delivery – to make the customer's experience a seamless one. The customer will feel appreciated and their needs will have been taken care of.

Ways to Add Value to Your Business

There are many ways to enhance your offer, depending on your budget and the resources you have access to. You may wish to hold a brainstorming session with your staff to come up with ideas for your business; if your employees are on the front lines, they'll likely have firsthand information about what clients would like to see more of.

Feature Your Expertise

Your intellectual property is a free resource that you have at your disposal to share with your clients. This will make them feel as though they have an inside track. You might want to consider adding it to your business, making it a value-added service.

Top Secrets to Create A Top Performing Business

Expert corner: Supplement your website and newsletter with columns on topics of interest to your customers and of relevance to your service. This will position you as an expert in the marketplace, and give your clients helpful information they won't receive from the competition.

Do It Yourself Tips: This is a great tool for seasonal marketing. Provide your clients with this information on your website, in your newsletters, or on take away note cards in your store or office. Ideas include recipes, craft ideas, gift ideas – all of which are branded with your company logo and contact information, and include your product as an ingredient.

What to Expect Tips: Take your customer through what they should expect in the first few days (weeks) of using your service or product, and how they can make the most of it. This can include assembly instructions, product care and cleaning, or service results (like a 25% increase in business – guaranteed!).

Related + Community Events: Own a store that sells athletic equipment? Post information on your website, in store, and in your newsletter about upcoming races, games, or consumer trade shows. Or simply keep a bulletin in your office of community events and offers that will draw your clients in, and establish itself as a hub in the neighborhood for information.

Top Secrets to Create A Top Performing Business

Offer Convenience Services

Customer service is a dying practice in our high paced culture – use it to your advantage. When done well, it can be the difference between you and the competition, or the deciding factor for a potential repeat client.

Envision the steps involved for a customer to arrive at your store, purchase your offering, and use your product or service. Can you eliminate any of those steps for them? Can you shorten waiting times, or make them more pleasurable? Stepping into your clients' shoes will allow you to determine the most powerful value add for your company. Here are a few ideas:

Free Delivery + Shipping: With clearly established parameters (will you ship your product free to India?), this is a solid value added service that many businesses offer. Free delivery (usually with a purchase over a set amount) is a huge convenience for many people who do not have access to a vehicle, or need help moving large items.

Follow up Services: This works great for computers, appliances and other mechanical or technology-based products. Offer maintenance and service contracts for three time periods; instead of dealing with the manufacturer, customers will rely on you for assistance which brings them back into the store and establishes a relationship of trust.

Gift-Wrapping: A great service to provide – especially for seasonal gifts. This service costs very little, and can have a big impact on your customer's experience.

"While You Wait" Amenities: If you could make your customer feel like a VIP for minimal cost, why wouldn't you? Offering amenities like coffee and treats, free samples and services (wireless internet is a big one) will go a long way.

Comparison-Shopping Tools: Show your customers that you are so sure your product will measure up against the competition, that you'll help them compare.

Establish Complementary Partnerships

Complementary partnerships with other businesses can take you a long way toward adding value for your customer, and generating new business. Just like a joint testimonial mailing, the power (and convenience) of referral business is immense.

Build a web of associates: If you're a yoga instructor, carry the cards of your treatment providers (physiotherapists, massage therapists, etc.) to refer your students to. In exchange, your brochure or card is posted in their offices. This works for automotive repair, esthetics, consultants and other service providers. Customers will trust referrals received by their existing service providers, and feel taken care of by a reputable community of experts.

Establish partnerships with financial incentives: This is one that has your interests in mind as well as your customers'. In addition to establishing a complementary partnership with a related associate, establish an incentive structure where each of you are compensated for your referrals. For example, if you refer a client to a furniture store after they've purchased a mattress from you, and they buy a bed frame, your associate will pay you a portion of the sale – and vice versa.

Location-based partnerships: Consider creating partnerships with the businesses around you – even if your products and services don't appear to be related. Shopping malls do this all the time with value coupon books that customers must purchase for $5 to $20 dollars. These partnerships and incentives will keep the customer spending money in the area, which is good for everyone's bottom line.

Packages + Bundles

Packaging and bundling products and services is one of the most popular methods of adding value. Clients perceive the bundles as having a higher value than the sum of the individual items – or as receiving something for free.

Cleverly packaged and named bundles can spark interest and revive your products in the eyes of your customers. Remember to always give the offers an end date or provide a limited number to create a sense of scarcity and urgency and to prevent this strategy from going stale.

Intuitive product bundles: Package independent related products together, and give them a reduced price or name. For example, this could be selling an extra pair of running socks with new running shoes. Remember the convenience of starter kits – package everything your customer will need to begin a new activity – painting, camping, running, etc. – in a bundle for simple buying decisions.

Package your upsell: This can also be called a chain of purchasing. It includes the products or services your client will need to use your product or service. Won't they need leather protector for their new boots? If they've run out of oil paints, how's their supply of brushes, acrylics or canvases? By packaging these clearly related products together, you are making their shopping experience faster and more convenient.

Top Secrets to Create A Top Performing Business

Offer a Customer Loyalty Program

There are a number of ways to structure your rewards and loyalty program, depending on the type of business and level of technological resources available to you. Customer loyalty programs have a huge advantage – they help build your database of customer information and in most cases allow you to view and analyze purchasing patterns. Here are the most popular:

Every 6th (or 10th) Visit on Us: This works well for business that rely on repeat visits from their customers – like hair salons, coffee shops, auto maintenance, etc. Customers receive a card with store information on the front, and space for stamps or initials on the back. Remember that while 10 is a nice even number, it may be too far in the future for some customers (especially for services that are three to six weeks apart). The idea of six visits is more manageable.

Rewards Dollars: This is the Canadian Tire model. For every dollar your customer spends in store, they receive a small portion back in store credit (i.e., Canadian Tire money). The store credit is in the form of printed dollars, branded with your company logo and contact information, and serves as a reminder each time a client opens their wallet.

Rewards Points: Another common value-add strategy is a rewards points system. Most grocery stores use this incentive, as well as credit card companies. This works the same as rewards dollars, where a certain number of points are accumulated based on each dollar spent in store. Points can then be spent in store, or on products you have brought in for "rewards points holders" only. This strategy also allows you to feature products with "extra points value" instead of discounting prices.

Membership Amenities: Instead of points or dollars, you can offer VIP treatment for members, when they sign up for or purchase a membership. This may include occasional discounts, but is primarily centered around perks like "while you wait" amenities, skipping the line, free delivery, etc. You can also produce membership cards.

So What Do You Do From Here?

So what do you do from here?

Take Action! If you're already an accomplished business owner and earning in excess of $250,000.00 per year (rich according to the Federal Government), use this book as direction to enhance the speed of your business success. If you are not as accomplished as you would like to be then the smartest thing to do is...

A)   LEARN
B)   PRACTICE
C)   EXECUTE
D)   REPEAT

Concentrate on strategies to LEARN and the EARN will follow! If you are serious about taking the next step then go to work on yourself, study other business successes, understand marketing strategies and become a sponge for new (proven) material. The amazing thing about the game of business is that when you put proven processes to work and continue to follow them, an abundance of success will follow. The biggest mistake is to start a process and then fallback into your old habits after a short time.

Above all, get the knowledge you need before you step onto the field. Think about it… if you were going to challenge Michael Jordan to a game of H O R S E for money, wouldn't it make sense to learn the game and practice before you stepped on the court to play him? It is amazing to me how many new small business people start the game of business against seasoned professionals (the competition), without first developing the necessary knowledge to be successful. Then they fail and blame the market, the economy, their location, etc.

If you have a business and have not yet managed to start to create wealth and systems that allow you to take time off, build retirement accounts or pay for your children's college, then learn and master the steps outlined in my book. I am a huge advocate of education and mentorship. Get the right information, find someone that knows how to walk you through them and watch your quality of life take new shape.

For a Free Test Drive of all my best tips, tricks and marketing resources, visit **www.Topchoicebusinessacademy.com**